THE GOD

you're

LOOKING FOR

THE GOD

you're

LOOKING FOR

BILL HYBELS

A
JANET
THOMA
BOOK

THOMAS NELSON PUBLISHERS
Nashville • Atlanta • London • Vancouver
Printed in the United States of America

Published in Nashville, Tennessee, by Thomas Nelson, Inc., Publishers, and distributed in Canada by Word Communications, Ltd., Richmond, British Columbia.

The Bible version used in this publication is THE NEW KING JAMES VERSION. Copyright © 1979, 1980, 1982, 1990 Thomas Nelson, Inc., Publishers.

Verses marked TLB are taken from *The Living Bible*, copyright 1971 by Tyndale House Publishers, Wheaton, IL. Used by permission.

Scripture quotations marked NIV are taken from the HOLY BIBLE, NEW INTERNATIONAL VERSION ®. Copyright © 1973, 1978, 1984 by International Bible Society. Used by permission of Zondervan Publishing House. All rights reserved.

Scripture quotations noted NASB are from the New American Standard Bible,© 1960, 1962, 1963, 1968, 1971, 1972, 1973, 1975, 1977 by The Lockman Foundation. Used by permission.

Library of Congress Cataloging-in-Publication Data

Hybels, Bill.
    The God you're looking for / Bill Hybels
      p. cm.
    Includes bibliographical references.
    ISBN 0-7852-7205-4 (hc)
    ISBN 0-7852-7107-4 (pb)
    ISBN 0-7852-7120-1 (Special Leather Edition)
    1. God. I. Title.
BT102.H93   1997
231—dc21   96-50118
                                     CIP

Printed in the United States of America.

2 3 4 5 6 — 02 01 00 99 98 97

DEDICATION

To my children, Shauna and Todd. If I could line up all the
daughters and sons in the whole wide world . . .
Dad
As always to the congregation
of Willow Creek Community
Church . . . What a ride!

CONTENTS

ACKNOWLEDGMENTS

Special thanks to Judson Poling for help with the manuscript.

DOES HE
OR DOESN'T HE?

◼

You are waiting behind a solid oak door as the clerk of the court makes sure everyone is present. With a nod of his head, the clerk pushes the door open and you notice the quiet, nervous fidgeting of the seated observers as you shuffle in. Glancing around, you perceive that the other jurors wear a look of resolution on their faces, and you wonder if your own countenance bears the same weariness.

The judge waits for you and the rest of the jurors to find your seats, then looks at the foreman. "Have you reached a verdict?" he asks.

"We have, Your Honor," the foreman replies.

The entire courtroom is focused on you and your colleagues. There is a sense of wonder and awe at what is about to take place. Each one of you—twelve in all—were handpicked by the defense and prosecution under the direction of sophisticated jury consulting firms. The lawyers found out which words would evoke which emotions out of which juror, and they have used this knowledge to present the best case possible.

◼

For your part, you and the jury have spent the last several days weighing the evidence, answering your own questions as well as the questions raised by your fellow jurors, and you have now reached a decision you will soon proclaim to the rest of the courtroom.

Though most of the jurors feel very confident about the decision you have reached, you are humbled when you realize that not a single one of you is *absolutely sure* about the verdict. But, remembering the judge's final instructions, you realize you don't have to be. Even in a trial that could speak life or death to the defendant, there isn't a single judge in this country who would ask a jury for absolute certainty. Our forefathers decided that to expect enough evidence in a trial to convince all the jurors beyond *any* doubt is as unreasonable as it is unrealistic. Life just doesn't work that way.

Living on the Edge of Probability

If you think about it, in almost every dimension of daily life, you make decisions based on high probability rather than con-clusive proof. Every day hundreds of thousands of people board an airliner for another city. Most everyone has made arrange-ments for their arrival—who will pick them up and when, how they'll reach their hotel, where they'll be staying—but nobody can know for sure that once the plane leaves the runway it will subsequently land at the intended destination. Over 99 percent of all flights do land where they're supposed to, so it's only nat-ural that most passengers assume a safe arrival. But terrorism and mechanical failure raise their ugly faces often enough to remind us that nobody who boards a plane can do so with absolute certainty.

Except in the field of math and formal logic, life must be negotiated on the basis of probability. Seldom do you enjoy the luxury of making decisions that are based on enough evidence to absolutely silence all skepticism.

Why else would your palms sweat on your wedding day? You can't be absolutely certain that your newly formed union will last over the long haul.

You cannot be absolutely certain that you will have a job tomorrow morning—what if a fire destroys the plant? What if a merger forces you out? You don't *really* know that the meat you're eating at that fast-food restaurant isn't spoiled and ready to deliver you a fine dose of ptomaine poisoning. All of us are forced to live with a measure of uncertainty, and we grow accustomed to weighing evidence, considering data, and making our decisions based on probability.

The same was the case in the trial that opened up this book, though admittedly, this trial was far different from any other. This trial did something that might shock some of you: It put God Himself on trial. It asked if He really exists. The questions have been out there for millennia, and now was as good a time as any to lay them to rest.

But, as in any trial, it must be understood from the very beginning that it is unreasonable to insist on absolute proof. A person ought to be able to say, "I am convinced beyond a reasonable doubt that God exists. The evidence is sufficiently compelling and the arguments are logical enough so that I must honestly conclude, using my best mental faculties, that there is a God."

Let's rewind the tape and review the evidence. You're a member of the jury. All of heaven and earth is waiting to hear your answer.

Show Me This!

The prosecuting attorney is a heavyset man with a slight southern accent, smoothed over by years of trying to make his voice sound appealing to diverse audiences. His rhetorical skills are polished, and he's got you and the rest of the jury pinned to the back of your seats with the weight of his questions.

His advantage? He doesn't have to prove anything. All he has to do is sow sufficient doubt, create enough questions so that it would be impossible for the defense attorney to answer them all, and then find that one stubborn juror who simply refuses to give in.

"All right," he says, "if God exists, explain to me how come thirteen innocent people were killed—including a baby—in last spring's tornado. If God exists, how come a young newlywed couple boarded TWA Flight 800 to celebrate their new life together, but the plane exploded in midair and they never made it?"

The attorney's cadence is staccatolike, and it cuts down the defenses of your fellow jury members as you sit mesmerized by his voice. "If God exists, how come cancer eats us from within at the same time that war and famine threaten us from without?

"How come?"

You notice that many members of the jury begin nodding their heads. The attorney's "how come" lingers in the air like a mist until he continues, "If God exists, why doesn't He answer all our prayers? If God exists, how come we can't agree on what He's like? Is He the nothingness of the Buddhists, the exacting God of the Muslims, or, as the Christians say, the loving Father of Jesus Christ? How can we possibly know who's right and who's wrong?

"If God exists, why are children born hungry, devout people buried poor, and good people stricken by fire and earthquakes? If God can't control the weather, the elements, or our society, how can He really be a god after all?"

A look of confidence and assurance covers the face of the prosecuting attorney as he scans the countenances of his twelve jurors. He knows he has done his job. He's argued the hope and the life right out of you—and how difficult was that, anyway? He knows each juror's history. He knows one of you had a mother die of Alzheimer's; another lost a child in a tragic car accident. He knows that two of you were forced into unemployment after eleven and twenty years of service, respectively. He knows one of you lost a relative in a California earthquake. He has played on your fears as a master violinist plays the strings of his instrument, and he now wraps up his argument before any of your doubts can be quelled.

"If God really exists," he concludes, "why do fewer people believe in Him than ever before? Why has it taken Him so long to convince us that He even lives? Why doesn't He just reveal Himself and remove all doubt—once and for all?"

He pauses until each juror's face is riveted to his. "In fact," he says, lowering his voice to almost a whisper, forcing you to pay attention, "if God exists"—then raising his voice to a shout—"why doesn't He strike me dead now for arguing against Him!"

You lean back in your seat in horror, almost waiting for the lightning to strike inside the courthouse. But nothing happens. The prosecuting attorney pauses to let you catch your breath, then steps back with a calm, self-satisfied smile.

"I'm still here," he says, "and that proves that God isn't." Turning toward the front of the courtroom, he nods at the judge and says, "Your Honor, I rest my case."

The Defense

The defense attorney, a professional-looking woman in her mid-forties, with close-cropped hair and glasses held around her neck by a chain, stands up and walks toward you.

"The only thing this man has proved," she states matter-of-factly, "is that we need a God more than ever. I can't make you see God. I can't parade Him in front of you so you can touch Him. I can't promise you that you'll hear His voice if you call out His name.

"But I can tell you that there are several reasons why you can trust the burning in your heart that already tells you God exists. These arguments may not stop the rain of your doubts from falling, but they will give you a roof under which you can stand."

Still stunned by the prosecuting attorney's explosive conclusion, you find yourself settling back into your seat, thankful for the reprieve provided by the calmness of the defense attorney.

"First—and I don't want this word to scare you—there is what historians have called the 'cosmological' argument. The word *cosmological* comes from two Greek words: *cosmos*, meaning world, and *logos*, which in this case means reason. Put this together and what do you have? The reason for the world.

"There are a number of variations on this argument, but this morning I'm going to put forward one that contains three different rationales. The first is called the principle of sufficient reasons. We begin with the undeniable assumption that something exists. Touch your arm."

Most members of the jury—including you—do so.

"You feel something, don't you? On your way to the courthouse this morning, as you walked outside, what did you see? Trees? Grass? Lake Michigan? The sun, maybe? I know this is Chicago, and this time of year we may even be wondering if the sun really exists. In fact, like many Chicagoans I have a bumper sticker on my car that states exactly how I feel about our weather—Have You Hugged Your Sump Pump Lately?"

You laugh. The attorney continues. "Whatever you feel about it, you cannot deny that Chicago weather exists. Some would say Chicago weather *happens*, but in any case, it's there and you feel it, don't you?"

You nod your head in agreement. "The cosmological question asks, '*Why* do things exist?' Suppose for a moment that nothing existed. Would nothingness require an explanation? Hang with me—I promise not to take you through the twilight zone! But clearly, nothingness requires no explanation. But the split second that something exists, in that millisecond we are forced to grapple with the question of *why*. Why does it exist? Why *something* rather than *nothing*?

"The second rationale—the 'principle of contingency'— relates to the need of everything for something else. Most everything is dependent on something other than itself. Trees need air, grass needs water, and the Chicago Bears need fans— not to mention a good quarterback, but we won't go down that road.

"Nothing is utterly independent or self-reliant. In fact, even the prevailing theories of cosmology confirm our observations. The big bang theory, for instance, says the universe at one time

did not even exist and probably will not continue to exist forever.

"The second law of thermodynamics teaches us that everything in our universe is in a gradual state of entropy—slowly
disintegrating, gradually losing energy and complexity. If you
doubt this, I'll have our researchers dig up one of your high
school graduation pictures, and we'll compare it with your most
recent driver's license. Even you are in a gradual state of
entropy!

"These first two rationales—that everything is dependent
on something else and that all is fading—lead us to the third
rationale: If all that exists is indeed contingent, who or what is
the explanation for all of these contingent objects and beings?
If everything is relying on something else, what is the basis that
supports the whole?"

The defense attorney walks up to the jury box, leans over,
and catches your eyes. "To put the question still another way: If
there was a big bang, who pulled the trigger?"

She walks over to a stand and removes a cover from a large
picture of the universe. "Take an imaginary journey with me
and pull yourself out of the universe for a second. Look at
everything that exists—imagine all the galaxies, the stars, the
planets, everything. Now"—she picks up a red marker pen—
"let's draw a circle around everything, and I mean everything.
We won't leave out the tiniest subatomic particle. We'll get
every quark and meson, and all the 'dark matter' scientists the-
orize is out there."

With her right hand, the attorney draws a circle around the
outside of the picture. "Now we have everything that exists in
the universe inside this circle. Everything inside this circle is
dependent on something else for its existence, and everything

inside this circle is slowly winding its way down. That," she says, looking at the prosecuting attorney, "is a statement of irrefutable fact.

"Now, the big question—the only question that really matters—is, What caused all this contingent stuff to exist in the first place? And second, What caused it to start winding down?

"The answer to this question logically must lie in only one of two places. The ultimate cause of everything must be located either inside the circle or outside the circle. There are no other options. So, what explanation makes the best sense?

"Certainly, it's not *inside* the circle. We've already discussed that everything there is contingent. If something is contingent, it's not self-reliant, so how can it have caused everything else?

"Doesn't a thinking person *have* to conclude that the explanation for all that exists inside the circle must lie *outside* the circle? If something is outside the circle, by definition it must be noncontingent, uncaused, self-reliant, wholly independent. To use other language, it would have to be eternal, unlimited, and all-powerful. And those kinds of adjectives come dangerously close to the classical definition of God."

"I object!" the prosecutor's voice thunders across the courtroom.

"Of course you do." The defense attorney smiles. She turns to the judge. "Your Honor, countless people have wrestled with this 'universe puzzle' over hundreds of years. They've studied it, dissected it, and debated it, and most have found that it makes logical, rational sense.

"In fact," she adds, "it makes far more sense than to suggest that because somebody doesn't strike you dead, he must not exist."

She pauses and turns her gaze to the prosecuting attorney. "If you object so much, why don't you slap me across the cheek?"

"I wasn't raised to treat a lady that way," the prosecuting attorney responds.

"You mean, it's against your nature?"

"I guess you could say that."

"Then maybe it's against God's nature to strike you dead capriciously, just because you don't believe He exists.

"Silence," she adds, "proves nothing."

"Objection overruled," the judge's monotone voice cuts in. "Counsel, you may proceed with your argument."

Designer Genes

"The first argument, the one historians have called the cosmological argument, looks at the cosmos and asks, 'Who put everything there?' The second argument is called the teleological argument, and it asks, 'Why is everything so ordered and complex?'

"Let me paint an illustration of this. If you went to Las Vegas and rolled one die, and got a one, you wouldn't be surprised. If you then rolled the die again, and got a two, you wouldn't have a second thought. But if the next time you rolled the die, you got a three, you might begin to wonder what was going on. And if you rolled it again and again, and got a four, five, and then six, you'd start to ask questions.

"If you kept rolling the die all day long and all day long the same pattern kept repeating itself, one-two-three-four-five-six, one-two-three-four-five-six, eventually you would stop and say, 'This can't be happening by chance. Somebody *has* to be playing a trick on me.' You would say this because you know that random chance can only go so far.

"For centuries, people looked at the complexities and wonders of the universe and simply assumed that a master designer was behind it all. Common sense told people this. This traditional thinking was basically unchallenged until the eighteenth century—somewhat ironically called the Age of Reason—when scientists began postulating that the origins of life could be explained by chance processes over long periods of time."

The attorney pauses to arrest your gaze, then asks, "Tell me this, how likely is it that a steel factory explodes and, amazingly, an automobile is created in the process? And what are the mathematical probabilities of a chance collision of floating gases eventually producing even a single living micro-organism, let alone a process as complex as photosynthesis or an action as breathtaking as an eagle in flight?

"Remember what the teleological argument basically says: The random chance explanation for the complexity and design and order of this world is highly, *highly* unlikely—so much so that it is unreasonable. The philosopher William Paley once wrote, 'There simply cannot be a design without a designer. There cannot be contrivance without a contriver. There cannot be order without choice.'

"Even Charles Darwin, the father of evolutionary theory, understood this. In *Origin of Species*, he admits, 'To suppose that the eye, with so many parts all working together, could have been formed by natural selection seems—I freely confess—absurd.'

"Well, he got one thing right. It *is* absurd. For those interested in numbers, one eminent scientist calculated the probability of the chance creation of a single protein molecule to happen once in ten to the 243rd power number of years. That's ten with two hundred and forty-three zeroes behind it—billions of trillions of years—for one, single protein molecule, let alone any type of life.

"When you consider the sheer physiological wonder of our eyes and ears, our skin, our sense of touch and smell, our emotional and mental capacities—well, it takes a lot more faith to see these resulting from a gaseous explosion than to believe we were custom-designed by God.

"Can you imagine a mother looking into the face of her newborn baby and saying, 'My, what a lovely collision of gases'? We no more expect such a lovely baby to be an 'accident' of nature than we expect a fabric store to blow up and have a pair of designer jeans pop out. Designer jeans were designed by somebody, they're not an accident, and we would never believe they could just 'happen.' Yet our genes are far more complex than a pair of designer pants."

Knowing she has the jury moving with her, the defense attorney picks up the pace.

Who Says?

"There's yet a third argument," she says, "a very simple one, actually. How is it that human beings everywhere, worldwide, recognize a common moral code?

"Think about it. If human beings simply evolved from primeval gases, if they are merely grown-up germs or recent improvements on bipedal hominids, how does one account for the fact that in almost every culture on the planet people value truth-telling over deceitfulness, kindness over violence, and loyalty over back-stabbing? Are gases, germs, or genes capable on their own of somehow creating a remarkably consistent code of values and implanting it in the minds and the hearts of billions of individual people?

"It amazes me that many of the atheists I meet are members of some humanitarian or charitable cause. It is utterly inconsistent for an atheist to believe we're all an accident and still care about what happens to others accidentally! By definition, an atheist is saying that we are not created beings made in the image of God and that we do not have a moral law stamped on our hearts. Yet at the same time, this atheist is trying to appeal to some code of morality—where did it come from, anyway, and why should I obey it?—to stop the 'savage' extermination of whales and to awaken people to the plight of the homeless.

"If we're all an accident, how am I to know that the homeless aren't just some unfortunate bump on the evolutionary scale, the antisocial who didn't quite 'make' it? And why should I care?"

I Know He Lives

"We're almost done," the attorney continues. "There's just one more argument I'd like to make, one that is far from being conclusive in and of itself. But when it's combined with the other arguments, it's very compelling. It's called the religious experience argument, and it's based on the notion that millions of trustworthy people have felt the presence of God, have sensed His direction in their lives, and have experienced His strength preparing them for some task.

"Certainly, it's very possible that a deluded or deceitful person might manufacture a claim to religious experience, but we're not talking about one or two or even a few hundred cases. We're talking about thousands of years of history in which some of our best and finest thinkers—well-adjusted, non-marijuana-smoking people all over the world—have borne witness to a real experience with God. Political leaders, chief justices, scientists, sociologists, economists, as well as honorable butchers, bakers, and candlestick makers. They all testify to feeling loved by God, and they claim to have received forgiveness from Him. Somehow they just *know* He's real because they've met Him.

"And while those of us who have a relationship with God treasure these experiences very much, the real question for you, the jury, is, How should we account for all of these Christians from very different cultures and sociological strata? Are hundreds of millions of Christians worldwide hallucinating? Are they lying? Can this honestly be dismissed as a well-organized conspiracy?"

The defense attorney wraps up her case. "I don't expect anyone to believe in the existence of God based on the religious argument alone, but considered with the others—that there must be some explanation outside of the universe for why everything exists; that there must be some designer behind such an intricately designed world; that there must be some author behind a remarkably consistent moral code—I think it's tremendously compelling."

But what about you?

■

The God You're Looking For

The defense attorney has stated her case and the evidence is laid in your hands. As the focus of the trial now shifts to you, the jury, you're called upon to make a decision. The answer may be more important—and far more urgent—than you realize.

You see, some day you will stand accountable for what you did with these evidences for the existence of God. You are going to have to answer for yourself, "What caused there to be something rather than nothing? What caused that something to be ordered? And what caused that ordered something to become 'someones'—people who have a sense of right and wrong? Finally, how is it that millions of these 'someones' claim to feel loved by God and to talk to Him?"

In fact, honest people everywhere admit to an occasional late-night, ceiling-staring session in which God visits them and says, not audibly but in their hearts, *Come on. Stop running. Stop pretending you don't need Me. Stop putting Me off as though I do not exist. Open up your heart to Me. Find out who I really am and what I am up to. Let Me show you what I could do in your life.*

The question for you right now is: How will you respond?

If you are already a Christian, please don't be embarrassed or shrink back from boldly proclaiming that you walk and talk regularly with a God who is there. You have no reason to cower when someone challenges your faith, because your faith is not based on shifting sand or mere wish-fulfillment. It has a strong foundation, a rational foundation, and a compelling foundation—logically as well as experientially.

I can safely assume that some of you reading these words are "seekers"—people concerned enough about the truth to take the time to read a book like this, but not yet certain enough to say, "I'm convinced beyond a reasonable doubt." Maybe you would describe yourself as "on the outside looking in"—that is, still in the process of weighing the evidence.

I have a suggestion for you. When God visits you the next time—and He *will* visit you—simply say, "Okay. I know You are real. Deep down I have known it all along. Please, God, forgive me for put-offs and time passed."

If you need to, feel free to add, "God, You are going to have to make Yourself known to me. Help me understand who You are. Help me better understand who Jesus is, and what He did for me on the cross; it doesn't make sense to me right now, but help me put the whole thing together in my mind so that I can understand and take action soon."

I suspect that the God I know is the God you're looking for. He's not the God of your nightmares. He's not the God of a screaming, overzealous evangelist. He's not the God who eagerly waits for you to fail so He can carry out His sentence of wrath with unbounded glee.

On the contrary, He's a God who wants to be in an intimate relationship with you. He's the God who has orchestrated every event of your life to give you the best chance to get to know Him, so that you can experience the full measure of His love.

I bet not one person in a million fully understands how much God loves him or her. One thing I can say for sure: God cares about you far more than you realize.

This is your invitation to find out. This is your chance to put aside the caricatures, the fears, the lies, and the misconceptions that have gathered over the centuries about who God really is.

But first, you have some unfinished business. How did you vote? Are you convinced of God's existence, and eager to get to know this God who you're now sure really exists? If so, hang on—you're going to find, as I have, that the very best part of believing in God is discovering how flat-out wonderful He is.

But perhaps you are still struggling with a few nagging questions. You may be saying to yourself, "You've made some good points, Bill, but . . ."

That's okay. Hang with me. The next step you need to take is to get to know the nature of this God who I—and millions of Christians like me—say exists. You may not believe in Him yet. But at least you owe it to yourself to get to know the *real* God of the Bible. Why? Because I believe, with all my heart, that the God I know and love is the God you're really looking for.

Read along with me, and see if you don't agree.

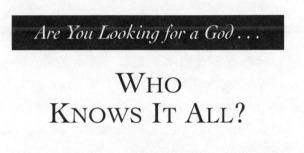

Are You Looking for a God . . .

WHO KNOWS IT ALL?

When I was in high school, once a year, for two solid weeks, every ounce of my strength was dedicated to one goal: making the basketball team. When I woke up in the morning, I thought about what I'd have to do in practice to impress the coach. At lunch, I'd think about what kind of food would allow me to play my best. As three o'clock drew ever closer, I found myself less able to concentrate on school and almost totally obsessed with getting mentally prepared for tryouts.

And every day, from three o'clock to five o'clock, thirty young men were "owned" by the basketball coach. He was the sun around which we orbited. If he told us to run lines until we thought our legs were going to fall off, we ran them, and then some. If he told us to ignore the blisters on our feet or the jammed fingers on our hands, we gritted our teeth and did so. If he told us we had to keep our hands up on defense, we did so until our shoulders ached from the exertion.

All our labors were centered on one thing: We wanted to make the team, and we were willing to sacrifice practically anything to do it.

Finally, near the end of the second week of tryouts, the coach gathered us around and gave his annual speech. "Boys," he said, "thirty of you are trying out for the team, but only eleven will make it. On Friday at 3:00, I'm going to post a list outside my office in the locker room. If you're on the list, you're on the team. If you're not on the list, you're not on the team. There won't be any typos or people accidentally left off that list, so don't even think about asking. Got that?"

Thirty heads nodded in unison.

"All right. You've got one more practice to convince me that your name should be on that list!"

Trying desperately to convince the coach of our worth, we spilled enough sweat in that one practice to fill a small pond. When five o'clock rolled around, there wasn't a guy in the gym who didn't feel as if his legs had been the victim of a sadistic contortionist. Our lungs burned, our eyes stung from the sweat that poured down our faces, and we limped toward the showers, wondering whether our efforts had been enough.

The next day, there was a major traffic jam outside the coach's office at three o'clock. Thirty boys, full of delirious hope and a good measure of dread, rushed over as soon as the bell rang. Only eleven would make the team. I remember walking up behind the crowd, seeing the hand-slapping, hearing the yells, but then also seeing the faces of the guys who walked silently and sadly away.

The crowd was so large I remember trying to read the list from ten feet away. In those situations, you ask your eyes to do the impossible: find your name immediately out of a list of eleven. You want your name to be the first one you see, for the eye-scroll down the line is an excruciating exercise for a hopeful young teen who is practically bursting with expectation, hope, and fear.

For an eternal ten seconds, you feel as though the only thing in the world that matters, the only thing that will matter for the rest of your life, is seeing your name on the list (fortunately, my name was on the list three out of four of my high school years).

Looking back on that time, almost thirty years later, I'm almost embarrassed by the significance of that roster, but at the same time, I'm frequently struck by the importance of another list—the one that holds the names of all those belonging to God. There will come a time when each of us will become acutely aware of that Final List. In that hour, we won't care how much money we made or how many times our name made it into the papers; we won't care what kind of houses we lived in or what kind of power we had or even how many thrills we experienced. The only thing that will matter is whether our name appears on that list.

And, like the basketball team, there is only one person who can put our name on that list. Our mother can't do it. Our best friends can't do it. Our pastor can't do it. Only the "Coach," God Himself, can do it.

Two types of people are going to be reading this book. The first group aren't even sure they believe in the Coach. To them, the Final List competes with Santa Claus and the Easter Bunny as cute little fairy tales that urge us to live more moral lives. But, just in case the Coach really does exist, they're willing to get to know what He would be like.

The second group, to varying degrees, are desirous or even desperate to please the Coach and make the team. Some in this group feel like veterans; they've played for the Coach for several seasons, and are already familiar with His pregame rituals, His personality habits, and what He really means when He clears his throat. Others are rookies. They've heard of the Coach, they've watched Him from a distance, but they have no idea what He's really like.

It might surprise you for me to say that all of you—seeker, rookie, and veteran—have essentially the same basic need. I was reminded of this when I heard a question thrown at a man I greatly respect. R. C. Sproul, a philosopher and theologian, was asked, "What, in your opinion, is the greatest spiritual need in the world today?"

Dr. Sproul paused, then replied, "The greatest need in people's lives today is to discover the true identity of God." He pointed out that most nonreligious people do not really understand the God they're rejecting. If they did, they would probably call a truce—at least a temporary truce—to make sure the battle was worth continuing.

Someone then asked the theologian a follow-up question: "What, in your opinion, is the greatest spiritual need in the lives of church people?"

To my delight Sproul shot back the very same answer: "To discover the true identity of God. If believers really understood the character and the personality and the nature of God, it would revolutionize their lives."

There you have it. The same thing that will feed the seeker will also help train the rookie and even hone the skills of the veteran: understanding the personality and nature of God. If we do this, Sproul says, it will "revolutionize" our lives.

Do you need a revolution? Are you a seeker who's never tried out for God's team? Or are you a Christ-follower who's just not making it as a Christian? Do you realize that simply improving one or two areas just won't do it? Could you use a complete overhaul?

Are you ready for a revolution?

That's what this book is really about. The power of Christianity is in the nature of the God we serve—yet most Christians barely understand God's true identity. Those who are still wondering if He's the God they're looking for know even less.

Fortunately, God does not keep His identity a cosmic secret. He doesn't play hide-and-seek, where the clues to His presence and nature are hidden behind distant planets or kept locked away in esoteric riddles. God announced Himself with an exclamation mark by proclaiming His nature in a type of autobiography, a book called the Bible. When we read His book and contemplate it over a period of time, we'll get an amazingly clear picture of who God really is—and our own lives will be set up for the most dramatic revolution we could ever imagine.

This chapter (and the next few) will deal with what are called "the omni's"—God's omniscience, God's omnipresence, and God's omnipotence. *Omni* just means "all," so what I'm talking about is how God is *totally* something—totally knowledgeable (omniscient), totally present (omnipresent), and totally powerful (omnipotent).

"I already believe all that," some of you might be saying. "Why do I need to read about it?"

Are you sure you believe it thoroughly? Does it affect the way you live your daily life?

Let's go back to my high school days for a moment. For two weeks, thirty high school boys' lives revolved around a crusty, hard-driving coach. His knowledge challenged us, his presence haunted us, and his power to choose us for the team humbled and at times humiliated us.

For fourteen days, that man changed every one of us. Granted, some of the changes were trivial and hardly life-changing—the way we shuffled our feet on defense, the follow-through after our free throws—but, in certain respects, you could say he "revolutionized" our basketball skills.

In the same way, God wants to revolutionize our lives—by showing us how knowing Him can be the most powerful force to help us become all we want to be.

Let's begin with an omni that might unnerve some seekers and casual Christians and at the same time provide unparalleled comfort for those who are deeply devoted to God—God's omniscience.

■

He Knows It All

When the Bible teaches that God is omniscient—that He has complete knowledge—it is not saying that God is bright. It is not saying that He is sharp. It is not even saying that He is a genius. These are the finite expressions of a people severely limited by space and time.

What the Bible is really getting at is that God knows *everything*. No question can confound Him. No dilemma can confuse Him. No event can surprise Him. He has eternal, intrinsic, comprehensive, and absolutely perfect knowledge.

Nothing is news to God.

■

But this knowledge extends even farther than today's events. God knows how *all* things work. Think about that. He has complete knowledge of all of the mysteries of biology, physiology, zoology, chemistry, psychology, geology, physics, medicine, and genetics. He knows the ordinances of heaven, as well as the reason and course for the sun and the moon and the clouds.[1]

And unlike anyone else, God's knowledge is not limited to time. He reads our future just as clearly as He reads our past. Who we will be fifty years from now is no less certain to God than who we were ten years ago.

Not only does God know why and how things work, but He also knows the minute details of their daily existence. Unlike a computer, He doesn't have any memory problems in which He is forced to flush His memory banks to create room for more information. Even though He keeps track of the moon and the stars, not a single bird falls to the ground without God knowing exactly what is going on.[2] His knowledge even covers seeming trivia, such as the latest count of the hairs on your head.[3] Hebrews 4:13 puts it this way: "All things are naked and open to the eyes of Him . . ."

Now, in this case, what is true of nature generally is true of you in particular. There isn't a single motivation, thought, act, or word that has slipped out of your being and escaped the full, undivided attention of God.

When we were trying out for the basketball team and happened to commit a turnover or blow a layup, the first thing we would do was look across the court to see where the coach's eyes were trained. Sometimes, we got away with an embarrassing mistake. Other times, however, we cringed when we realized the coach missed one of our best moves.

That won't happen with God. And the beauty of this truth is so stunning that it almost silences one of the most brilliant wordsmiths in all of Scripture, a man who lived three thousand years ago yet knew the same God I know, the same God you may be looking for: King David himself.

Amazed

Though many of the Psalms start out with a robust, "Bless the LORD," or "Praise the LORD," or "Rejoice in the LORD," in Psalm 139 David's knowledge of God's omniscience is so overwhelming, he manages only a whisper of wonderment: "O, LORD."

It's as if he is admitting right from the start that words won't be able to convey even a fraction of the power of this truth. His "O, LORD" is a verbal shrug of the shoulders: "How can I express this?" David could rejoice in the power of God, he could celebrate the beauty of God, he could delight in the provision of God, but when it came to the intimate way that God desired to know David inside and out (the type of intimacy that each one of us longs for but often becomes hardened toward as relationship after relationship breaks down), when it came to *this* kind of passion, words utterly fail David. The mighty warrior is defeated. The lyrical poet is speechless. The mighty king has lost his composure. He's stunned.

"O, LORD."

No flowery language here. No elaborate metaphors will do. Only a direct description of an amazingly powerful truth will suffice, for there is no analogy to match it. The truth itself seems too wonderful for words, so David simply gets out: "You have searched me and known me."

What has David so overwhelmed is his keen understanding that God's omniscience focuses and specializes on God's knowledge of *him*. Yes, God understands the intricate mysteries of the atom and the complex interconnectedness of our planetary system, but all that pales in comparison with David's understanding that God knows *him*. "You have searched *me*. You have known *me*."

This knowledge stretches even to the humdrum of our daily lives, such inane activities as sitting and rising: "You know my sitting down and my rising up."[4] God doesn't miss it. He's interested. Cross your legs, and God takes notice because we're the object of His knowledge.

"You understand my thought afar off." God knows everything we think. Every midnight musing, every calculating strategy, every private worship time, every act of kindness. God sees it all. We never have to look toward the sidelines to see if God's eyes are open or preoccupied somewhere else. They are always trained exactly on us, and God never blinks. You've never had a thought that God didn't know all about.

Then, in Psalm 139:3, David recognizes that *God follows our ways*. "You comprehend my path and my lying down, / And are acquainted with all my ways." God keeps a copy of our itinerary before it's printed. We have never taken a trip that has escaped His notice. If we're on top of the Sears Tower or buried in the mass of humanity traveling underground in the New York subway, God keeps His eyes trained on us.

God also knows what we say: "For there is not a word on my tongue, / But behold, O LORD, You know it altogether" (v. 4). Even before we say it, God charts our words and even the feelings that eventually lead to words. Think about that—God monitors our temperature! He feels the anger rising, He notices the fear spreading, and He sees the trust moderating. Good or bad, God sees it all.

But even more wonderful, David points out, *God knows what we need.* In verse 5, he states, "You have hedged me behind and before, / And laid Your hand upon me." This is a perfect kind of protection in which all my needs are known. If I'm thirsty, God knows it. If I'm lonely, God feels it. He's not like a lottery winner who shuns his friends in the time of their greatest need. On the contrary, in the midst of my needs, *He lays His hand upon me.* How do you like that? A God who promises to draw especially close just before a need presents itself!

And now, I believe, David is so overwhelmed he is forced to lay his pen down. His hand is shaking, his eyes are tearing, and his spirit is bursting. Finally he manages to scribble out verse 6—"Such knowledge is too wonderful for me; / It is high, I cannot attain it."

"If I wrote anything else," David seems to say, "it would just be profanity. I can't get on the page what it feels like to be in a relationship with a God who is so intimately acquainted with all my ways. It is too wonderful for me."

Israel's greatest conqueror admits defeat. "I better just lay my pen down, take off my shoes, and stand humbly on holy ground."

I've felt that way at times. Have you? Do you wish you had? This moment calls for worship, for surrender, for adoration. That's what David finds himself doing. Worshiping. He is shaken by an exhilarating implication, one that I hope every reader of this book will take away. If I am the object of such sovereign scrutiny, there is only one conclusion that I can draw: *I must really matter to God.* And a God who cares that much is the God I'm looking for.

This God doesn't scrutinize the trees as He scrutinizes me. He doesn't get intimately acquainted with the ways of rocks or bushes. He gets intimately acquainted with me because He is passionately moved by who I am.

That thought should bring all of us to our knees.

One Sunday a woman stopped me in the hallway after church. As we started talking she lost her composure, broke down, and threw her arms around me. "Don't ever stop telling us that we matter to God because it's changed my life."

"I won't," I said, "because it's changed my life, too, and it's still changing my life today."

The Bad News: He Knows Your Secrets

While David is overwhelmed at the thought of God's omniscience, I know that some of you might be shifting a little uneasily in your seat. Your collar may be feeling a little tight right now, and you might be wondering who turned up the heat.

How do I know that?

I've been there.

You see, when I ponder the fact that God knows all about me, I have to admit that, at times, such attention is a bit of a mixed blessing. The good news is: He must really care about me to want to know me so well. The bad news is: If He is intimately acquainted with all my ways, that means He is intimately acquainted with all my sin.

And that can be terrifying.

When I was a boy growing up in Michigan, my dad's produce company purchased a farm just outside of Kalamazoo. Every day, I'd wait for my father to come home from work, and when his car drove up, I'd rush to accost him, standing so close to the car door that he couldn't open it without bumping me. As soon as the door was opened a crack, I'd begin pleading, "Dad, let me ride my bike from school over to the farm, and you can teach me how to drive the tractor. Pleeeease?"

There was nothing I wanted to do more than to disk and drag a field with the tractor. My idea of heaven was sitting in that seat, starting the engine, and driving up and down the field until the sun went down.

"You're a little young, aren't you?" my dad would respond.

"I can do it, Dad, I know I can. Just give me a chance, pleeeease?"

Finally, he agreed to meet me at the farm. He explained how to start the engine, where the clutch and transmission were, and how to hook up the equipment and work the hydraulics.

I couldn't wait. To me, happiness was spelled J-o-h-n D-e-e-r-e, and I was about to drive it.

After my first lesson, my father walked me over to the gas pump. "One cardinal rule—and don't you *ever* break it—is never put gas in a hot tractor. When you are done and you need to refuel this thing, you bring it in and shut it off in front of a gas pump. Then, take a walk, go to sleep on a bale of hay, do whatever you want to do, but don't you try to put gas in a hot tractor. It can catch fire."

"No problem," I said as I nodded my agreement. And with my private lessons completed, I was off on an agricultural adventure.

For weeks, I would jump on my bike after school and ride to the farm, eager to drive that tractor. I had great fun disking and dragging the field. I even learned how to unhook the equipment at the end of the day, get the tractor going fast, then jam on one of the brakes, causing the tractor to spin around in circles. My brother proudly showed me how to rev the engine and pop the clutch so the front tire would jump off the ground. Life just didn't get any better than this!

One day I was particularly eager to finish a field when I looked at the fuel gauge and noticed that it was almost empty. My heart was set on finishing because I knew how proud it would make my dad. If I waited until the tractor cooled to refuel it, however, I wouldn't have time. I drove to the gas pump and ignored my dad's warning: "Never gas up a hot tractor."

He'll never know, I reasoned. In fact, to make it go even a little faster, I didn't even bother to shut the tractor off! Instead, I climbed up on a little stepladder and started pouring gas into the tank that was located right over that hot engine.

Then disaster struck. My foot slipped off the ladder. Gas spilled all over the engine, and suddenly a ball of fire shot up from the tractor, the explosion pushing me backward. I tumbled onto the ground, shocked and terrified at what I had done. I got up and watched in horror as flames engulfed the tractor and eventually melted the tires right in front of my eyes.

"I'm a dead man," I said to myself.

The bike ride home felt as if it was five hundred miles long. I looked cautiously into the driveway and was relieved when I noticed my dad's car wasn't there. When I walked into the house and inquired as casually as I could, I discovered he wouldn't be back for several days.

At first, I thought I was the luckiest kid in Michigan. But after a while, the wait became excruciating. *I'm going to have to tell him when he comes back home,* I kept thinking, and the imagined punishments that would surely follow grew worse and worse with time.

Finally, my dad came home, but my fear had reached such a pitch I couldn't bring myself to say anything. Earlier, I had talked about nothing but that stupid tractor, and now I practically broke out in hives if anyone so much as mentioned the word.

I finally decided to take the diplomatic approach and ignore the problem. *I'll wait until he brings it up*, I reasoned. *Who knows? Maybe he'll never find out.*

After dinner a few nights later, my dad opened the freezer and took out a half gallon of ice cream. He started scooping it out for us. He gave two scoops to my mom, two scoops to my brother and sisters, and then he came to me.

One scoop.

I looked at him and thought, *He shorted me . . . he knows!*

Even though I was eating ice cream, I could feel the sweat beading up on my forehead. *I've got to tell him*, I thought. *He already knows, anyway. Every minute that I hold out is nothing less than open treason.*

After dessert was over I went bursting into the family room. "Dad, I blew it. I filled up the gas tank while the motor was still running and burned the tires right off the tractor. If you want me to spend the rest of my life paying for the tractor, I will. And I promise never to do it again."

"Come over here, Son."

I slowly walked up to my dad and he took me gently into his arms. "I gave you those instructions because I didn't want you to get hurt. Next time, listen a little better, will you? Now, don't worry about it. The tractor was insured, and we've already replaced it. It's over. Just be there Monday, ready to work again."

When I left that room, I had an entirely new understanding of the theology of confession and forgiveness.

Some of you are involved in things God wants you to have no part of. You are guilty. You know you have violated God and the teaching of the Bible. You may be the only human being on the face of this earth who knows about your sin—but let me give you some news that is as good as it is sobering.

You don't have to spend anxious nights wondering when God is going to "find out." He already knows. You might pretend that He doesn't, but He does. Don't bother trying to perpetuate the sham.

It's over. He knows.

"All right," you might respond, "then what does God want from me?"

Simply this. He wants you to stop the cover-up. Come clean and agree to change your ways. He's not going to condemn you; He simply wants to liberate you from the guilt that you have carried and set you on a new course. Since He already knows all about it, what could possibly stop you from owning up to your sin and asking Him to forgive you?

Like me, some of you need to burst into your Father's "family room" and say, "Dad, I blew it. I really blew it," and then wait to hear His answer.

Some of you are going to be shocked, because you're going to find out that while He knows all about your sin, He still loves you. His reply is not all that different from my dad's: "It's over. Just start again in a different way . . . and I'll help."

That's what the God I know says to me. That's the good news, despite the bad.

And there's more good news concerning God's omniscience: He not only knows about your sin, He also knows all about your scars. In other words, He not only knows what you've done, He also knows what's been done to you.

The Good News: He Also Knows Your Scars

Every person is wounded in one way or another. As I grow older I am becoming ever more convinced of that. It is amazing how many people have shattered self-esteem. And when we talk about it, they say, "If you knew what went on in my home, if you only knew how I was treated growing up . . ." Or, "If you knew the violence my dad did to my mom," or "If you knew the alcoholism and how it affected our family . . ."

And of course I don't know, I can't know, but God does. He was there, and He didn't miss a millisecond of what took place.

Scars aren't just from childhoods. Some of you have more recent wounds, ones that are perhaps still too tender to be called "scars." They're open, bleeding wounds. A number of you are bleeding emotionally and spiritually because your dreams have been shattered. You've experienced business failures or suffered through agonizing days and nights that ended in a bitter divorce. Some of you have known the horror of losing a child to a terminal illness or tragic accident. Others might be suffering from relational failures, academic failures, financial debacles—you name it.

It's frightening how many people are walking around with shattered spirits. This past week, at the health club, a guy recognized me and said, "You're the pastor at Willow Creek."

As we started talking, it was obvious he was sad about something, so I asked him, "What's going on?"

"I buried my mom this afternoon. I've just come from the funeral . . . She was way too young."

For many of you, the walls feel as though they're mercilessly closing in. You may even hear your own screams and moans of agony echoing and bouncing off those walls, mocking you, taunting you, and making you feel even worse. "My spouse doesn't know what I'm feeling. Even worse, he doesn't want to know." "My parents couldn't care less if I disappeared tomorrow. Nobody would miss me."

Those of you who have screamed these screams need to be reminded of some powerful truths.

First, you must grab hold of the secure lifeline provided by the truth that *God knows.* He is *intimately* acquainted with all your ways. He doesn't watch you from a distance. No feeling, no hurt, no scar, no wound has ever escaped His notice.

Not only does He know, He cares. The Psalms declare, "You have seen me tossing and turning through the night"—let this next phrase sink in—"You have collected all my tears and preserved them in your bottle! You have recorded every one in your book."[5]

In ancient Middle Eastern culture, when a soldier went off to battle he would buy a "tear vial"—a little tear bottle—and he would give it to his wife or his mother. She would promise, "Your absence will make me so sad, I will cry every night. And when I do, I'll collect those tears in this bottle. When you come back, you'll see my tears and you'll know how precious you are to me."

How do you like that? When God greets us in heaven, He'll be able to wave our tear bottle in front of His smiling face. "Didn't miss a one," He'll say. "Not a single one."

Additionally, He not only collects each tear but also records each one in a book: "And I've written them down in My book." God is never careless with your tears, hurts, and wounds. That's how much you matter to Him.

With a love as observant and tender as that, surely God has earned the right to say, "I am intimately acquainted with all your tears and scars."

This is the God of the Bible, the God Jesus wants you to meet, the God you're looking for. You need never cry alone. Never.

Slowly but deliberately, take refuge in the omniscience and the compassion of God. Say it out loud if you have to: "I know Someone knows. And I know Someone cares."

Now another piece of wonderful news: God's omniscience means that He knows about our secret acts of service.

More Good News: He Knows Your Service

If I made a long-distance shot at basketball tryouts, but the coach never saw it, it was like it never happened. It didn't do me a bit of good. If I made a great defensive play, but his attention was occupied elsewhere, I realized that, in a sense, I had wasted my efforts. It wouldn't help me make the team.

Even today, sometimes I get discouraged because what I do doesn't seem to get noticed or appreciated. And the awful, soul-maddening silence that follows my secret acts of service often tempts me to conclude, "What's the use? Why bother being the Boy Scout? Who really cares? Nice guys finish last, anyway."

That's when I need this reminder: "Your Father who sees in secret will Himself reward you openly."[6] God is the note-taking heavenly observer. He knows about the time you bit your tongue when you could have contributed to a rumor. He takes notice every time you greet a stranger or visit a person in the hospital or prison. Every secret act of character, conviction, and courage has been observed in living color by our omniscient God.

You always have an audience. In every activity and in every conversation God is present, and He says, "I saw it. Carry on!

Do it again! I am going to reward you. I am going to repay you. You have not been working in vain."

Obviously your good deeds won't make God love you more (His love for you is operating at "full strength" already), but it's good to know He celebrates your good deeds—even when they go unnoticed by others.

Finally, God's omniscience can instill you with a supernatural confidence that can transform your life. If you can grasp this, it will flood your spirit with a divine courage to face life's greatest challenges.

■

Supernatural Confidence

When I was first learning how to sail my dad's sailboat out on Lake Michigan, he would often say to me, "Go ahead and take the boat out, but take a friend with you."

A forty-two-foot sailboat on a body of water the size of Lake Michigan is a big responsibility. But always up for a challenge, I'd find a junior high friend to accompany me and we'd sail past the breakwater, hoist the sails, and head out to open water. But as soon as I'd see any cloud formation coming our way or the wind seemed to be piping up, I'd head back toward shore, take the sails down, and regain my normal breathing pattern only when we were safely tied up in the slip. Most of the time, it was fun having a friend along, but in a storm, I knew this kid wouldn't be much help.

Other times, however, my dad would come home from work and we'd go out together. When I was sailing with my dad, I'd actually *look* for cloud formations and hope for heavy air. I loved the feel of strong winds and huge waves!

■

My dad had sailed across the Atlantic Ocean. He had endured five days of sailing through a hurricane. He was a veteran, and I was confident that he would be able to handle anything Lake Michigan could throw at us. Everything changed when my dad was on board.

We can have an even greater confidence with our heavenly Father. When you begin to know the omniscient God, you'll develop a supernatural confidence, even during the storms of life.

The omnipresence of God is powerful stuff. It makes ordinary people extraordinary, weak people strong, insecure people models of confidence and courage. There's not much you can't achieve or endure if you know God is walking by your side. Just remember: Someone knows and Someone cares.

I spoke earlier about the need for a "revolution." By that I mean it is high time to declare war on your ignorance of God's identity. Your lack of knowledge has probably kept you too defeated and too timid for far too long. It's time to break out of your self-imposed limitations and become the person you are capable of being.

God's omniscience is just one of the "amazing omni's." If you've been encouraged and strengthened by it, get ready. There's lots more to come. The revolution has just begun.

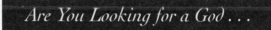

Are You Looking for a God . . .

WHO IS ALWAYS THERE WHEN YOU NEED HIM?

"Daddy?"

A little hand patted my forehead. I opened my eyes, which just happened to be trained on the digital clock in our room.

2:45.

That would be A.M., judging by the fogginess in my head.

"Yeah, Todd?"

"I need to go to the bathroom."

Todd was just five years old at the time.

"Fine, Todd. Thanks for the update. Go."

The bathroom was at the other end of the house—down a dark hallway. When you're five years old, it looks like it's about five miles long with multiple side rooms in which monsters and wild animals are just waiting for some poor little kid to pass by.

Todd dutifully shuffled out my door, took a few steps down

the hallway, and realized that the hallway was getting even darker as he walked. And what was that noise? And was that a shadow, or was something moving?

He quickly turned around. Shuffle, shuffle.

"Dad?"

"Yeah, Todd?"

"Why don't you come with me?"

"Thanks for the invitation, Todd, but I'm tired for some reason. You go ahead. Don't let me stop you."

Shuffle, shuffle. Stop. Turn around. Shuffle back.

"Daaaad?"

"Yes, Todd?"

"I really think you should come with me."

"Are you scared?"

"Noooooo. I just want you to walk with me, Dad. I just want you to walk with me."

"Okay." I jumped out of bed, and we walked down the hall together.

I don't know what *your* long, dark hallway is right now. Maybe you're embarking on a new business opportunity. If you hit a home run, all your dreams will come true. If you strike out—well, you'll lose your savings, your car, your house, everything.

Maybe you're facing a lawsuit. Maybe you're terrified at the thought of bringing a new baby home or watching your last child go off to college. Maybe you're being forced to walk down the darkened hallway of unemployment, an experimental medical treatment, or a disappointing family relationship.

Whatever your hallway is, what do you need more than anything else? Someone who is always by your side.

■

Someone Who Is Always There

Think back with me to the opening of the National Football League season in 1996. History was made by the Dallas Cowboys when one of their players, Deion Sanders, did something that has rarely been done since the early days of professional football. He started playing both defense (cornerback) and offense (wide receiver), frequently logging over one hundred plays in the same game.

It was amazing to watch. On one play, during the third game of the season, Deion even blitzed a run and stopped the running back behind the line of scrimmage. When Dallas got the ball back, he suddenly became a deep threat for a long pass from quarterback Troy Aikman.

"He's everywhere, friends! He's all over the field!" the announcers declared.

Now, Deion wasn't *really* everywhere. If you left your seat to buy a hot dog, Deion wouldn't have been working the concession stand. If you had to get out of the stadium early, Deion wouldn't have been directing the traffic.

But in hyperbolic language, the sportscaster was expressing the notion that Deion was covering an amazing amount of territory—something football fans hadn't seen in years.

What does Deion Sanders have to do with your long, dark hallway? Simply this. When we talk about the omnipresence of God, we're not using the hyperbolic language of a sportscaster. The omnipresence of God is literally true—wherever you are, God is. Whatever hallway you're in—no matter how long, how dark, or how scary—God is right there with you.

And that's exceedingly important information when you're facing your long, dark hallway.

■

But for some reason, it's a truth that is very difficult for us to accept.

Perhaps because we live in the age of the computer chip, we can readily imagine God being all-knowing (omniscient). After all, science fiction novels are filled with supercomputers that run the universe. It's not that difficult for us to believe that something—or someone—is actually capable of containing all the knowledge of the world.

But omnipresence—the concept that God is everywhere— is a little more difficult for us to grasp. That's something that even a supercomputer could never accomplish. What, exactly, does it mean?

The Bible says that God is Spirit, so technically, He doesn't dwell in three-dimensional space as we do.[1] His *presence* is everywhere, but not His *essence* (that would be the heresy known as pantheism). God is no less present in one portion of the universe than any other. And He is no more present any- where than where you are right now. In other words, anyone, anywhere in the universe might say, "The Lord is in this place." Wherever you are, God is right there, right now.

One evening about midnight I was in a private plane, flying over the cornfields of Iowa. Lightning streaked the sky at various places along the horizon, and after it had flashed, its fleeting bril- liance made the pervasive darkness seem all the more black. It was just me, the storm, and a fuselage made of metal—and a great big ever-present God. But I remember: I didn't feel frightened. I had a quiet confidence that assured me, "The Lord is in this place."

A man in my church sailed twenty-four hundred miles from Hawaii to San Francisco. One night, as forty-foot rollers sent his boat soaring as high as the roof of a suburban office building,

■

he was able to take great comfort in the fact: "The Lord is in this place."

When three astronauts from *Apollo 13* were caught in a broken-down spacecraft, hurtling around the moon to ride an orbit back to earth, whether they realized it or not, they could take confidence in the fact: "The Lord is in this place."

Of course, not everyone believes this. In fact, a number of years ago, some Russian cosmonauts traveled into space, and when they got back declared to the Russian people, "We went out to space and we didn't see God. He isn't there."

They might have been competent pilots, but they were amateur scientists. Did anyone think of asking them, "Did you happen to 'see' the solar wind? How about gravity? No, you didn't see them? I guess they don't exist either."

Behind the moon, behind the boardroom wall, behind your bedroom door—it doesn't matter. God is there. The Bible teaches that God is an "everywhere-present" God. And in case you think this is a meaningless, irrelevant theological technicality, just wait until you consider the implications.

■

More Than a Forgiver—A Friend

My upbringing stressed the transcendency of God. I thought of Him in lofty terms, especially the distance and otherworldliness of God—so much so, that at times it felt as if He was far removed from where I was. I understood what it was to fear God and I knew how important it was to serve Him. I knew that someday I'd stand under His judgment so I needed to learn how to obey Him. But with all that, one thing was sorely missing.

I realized this as I sat in the back of a college classroom one day and listened to one of my professors, Dr. Gilbert Bilizikian, talk about his relationship with Jesus Christ. Dr. B., as he's affectionately known, talked as if he had just had lunch with Jesus. Whenever he referred to Him, in fact, he reminded me of the way people speak of their closest friends—as if you could just walk and talk with Jesus.

I had studied under this professor long enough to know that he had a properly high and exalted view of God, but what intrigued me was his uncanny ability to relate to God in almost a brother-to-brother way. I wanted that more than I wanted anything else, so I stayed after class one day and asked him bluntly, "How is it that you know Christ in such a personal way and I don't?"

He paused and looked at me, then said something that caught me off guard. "Maybe you only understand Jesus as the forgiver of your sins."

As I thought about it, he was right. I had asked Jesus to forgive my sins. I had vowed to make Jesus the leader of my life. But nobody had talked to me about the role that Jesus covets most: to be my friend.[2]

And therein lies the most amazing news about Christianity: It's not just that God exists—other religions teach that. It's that God passionately yearns to be in a *loving relationship with the people He created.*

At first glance, that might not mean much to you, but it's a fact that has changed my life. I can divide my spiritual journey into two distinct eras: the first era, when I thought of God in nonrelational ways; and the second, when I began knowing Him and relating to Him more personally.

CEO Christianity

The *existence* of God was very easy for me to believe. Growing up, no one I knew or respected questioned that God existed—or at least no one let on if he or she did. But my concept of God was unidimensional. I saw Him as the "CEO of the universe." Christianity, I thought, was about learning the list of duties and prohibitions that the CEO had set in place. It was made very clear to me that there were consequences and rewards associated with carrying out the CEO's program for the world. What was required of me were the same two things required of most employees: to show up and to perform. So I went to church with my family and tried my best to follow and obey the CEO's agenda.

In many ways, you will find "CEO Christianity" to be remarkably similar to the major world religions, such as Islam, Buddhism, and Hinduism. They also have an impersonal dynamic with their deity, one completely devoid of tender feelings. There are beliefs to be mastered and codes to be followed and rituals to be engaged in, and at the end of the day, every good deed is added to the plus side of the scoresheet and every misstep causes a deduction—and hopefully you come out feeling good about yourself.

These religions tend to emphasize two things: belief and performance. What they lack is what makes Christianity unique: the realization that God has a genuine, passionate affection for each of us and invites us to open our hearts to that love and then return love to Him with deep sincerity.

Before Dr. B. challenged my limited understanding of God, I was doing all the mechanical parts of Christianity, but I lacked that kind of glow that marks someone who has come to know Jesus as a friend. I had a lot of head stuff going on in my faith, but not a lot of heart stuff.

So over the next few months and years, I started reflecting on the fact that our loving God is always present—in every conversation, in every relationship, in every seemingly solitary moment.

Christ-Centered Christianity

Let's face it. We're all relational beings. God created us to thrive on companionship. Kids as young as three years old start asking their parents, "Can Johnny spend the night?" Adolescents are obsessed with finding "the one." Middle-aged adults love to go out to dinner. And few things put a smile on an elderly person's face like the appearance of grandchildren or a lifelong friend.

Honest-thinking people, however, understand that even the best of friends cannot meet our yearning for the ultimate friendship. If you're in touch with your feelings at all, you have a yearning to know a companion in the ultimate sense of the word. But perhaps this has been a bittersweet recognition. You've come to realize that even best friends can't be around you all the time. Lifelong friends still move away or die. The most understanding of friends can't always comprehend what you're going through. And even the most trusted of friends don't always prove dependable.

Well, you ask, what kind of God would make us yearn for significant relationships but then deprive us of that very thing? To which God smiles and replies, "I know you have that yearning and I have supplied a way to satisfy your need. I offer you *Me*. I'm the ultimate companion."

This reality—that God is always present as my friend—has marked my life ever since my class with Dr. B., and in the rest of this chapter, I'm going to discuss the difference that the omnipresent God can make in your life as well. The first thing

I discovered by contemplating the presence of God was a radically new way to view my moral choices.

■

Looking Up

The Bible tells us Moses saw an Egyptian brutally mistreating an Israelite, and he had just about had enough, so he looked left, then right—didn't see anyone—and proceeded to murder the Egyptian and bury him in the sand.

What made Moses think he could get away with this homicide? He mistakenly thought the coast was clear. He looked every way but up.

That's what happens when we live without the conscious awareness of the presence of God. Hypocrisy is born in compartmentalization—we leave God in church and think He doesn't accompany us throughout the week.

A similar scenario developed with King David, as recorded in 2 Samuel. While Bathsheba's husband was off fighting a war, David spotted this beautiful woman taking a bath. In a matter of moments, his moral compass spun out of control and he took her into his bed, and then, when she got pregnant and David feared getting "caught," he ordered her husband to be killed in battle.

What was David thinking? *No one knows what goes on behind closed doors?* Wrong! God sent a prophet to set David straight, and maybe it was after this experience that David wrote: "Where can I go from Your Spirit? / Or where can I flee from Your presence?"[3]

An out-of-the-way hotel room? A bar down the street when you're away on a business trip?

That's not what David found.

If I ascend into heaven, You are there;

If I make my bed in hell, behold, You are there.[4]

David found that there was nowhere he could flee from God's presence. Do you have that awareness?

We're driving our cars. The posted speed is a paltry 55 mph. We know that in Romans 13 and other passages God has commanded us to obey the civil laws. But an important business meeting starts in ten minutes and we're twenty minutes away.

What do we do?

All too often, we look left, we look right, we glance at the radar detector—and then we consider the speed limit a mere suggestion for the other guy. We reason, "The coast is clear. Nobody sees this."

God does. "Even the night shall be light about me."[5]

If we live our lives without an intense awareness of the omnipresence of God, we create one illusion after the next. We start to think, *No one witnesses the way I "shade the truth" with a client in my office—they just hear me sing along with everybody else on Sunday morning.* Or, *No one witnesses my pilfering or "borrowing" of company pens and notepads—they just see me soliciting donations for the food bank. No one witnesses my 11 P.M. binge—they just see the disciplined portions I take at dinners out. No one hears how I raise my voice at my wife, my husband, or my children—all they hear is how well I pray at church. No one sees the illegal deal I am cutting—they just see the folded check I drop into the offering.*

Some of you are thinking, *I hate this! God is like Big Brother looking over my shoulder all the time, ready to jump on me for one wrong move.*

Not so. God does not hover over us to accuse us. He does it to improve our lives. He says, "Look, I want to hold you accountable. I want you to know you are never going to fool Me so give up those silly games and let's get on with it."

The first implication of God's omnipresence, then, is that we must never play games with ourselves, pretending that the coast is clear. That's the implication that seized David's attention. The next one makes his heart burst with joy.

The Hand of Love

Once David gets over the recognition that the coast is never clear, he overflows with joy. Psalm 139:7–12 could almost be summarized this way: "God is so remarkable and I matter to Him so much that if for some crazy reason I decided to try to run away from Him—it would be a stupid thing to do, but let's just say I tried it—I couldn't do it. God wouldn't let me. I'll never be out of His sight."

In verse 8, paraphrased, David says: "Let's say I went infinitely up. Or let's say I went infinitely down. God would be there.

"Or let's say I take off sailing in an easterly direction and sail on indefinitely."

God would be there.

But verses 9 and 10 lead us into even more comforting territory. David recognizes that God's presence isn't with us in a cold, calculating manner. His presence is warm and inviting and reassuring.

> If I take the wings of the morning,
> And dwell in the uttermost parts of the sea,
> Even there Your hand shall lead me,
> And Your right hand shall hold me.

Wherever I go, David says, I can feel His hand. This fatherly, reassuring kind of touch is available constantly to every single believer.

Many years ago, our family went to Disney World. Our son Todd was six years old at the time, the age when young boys want to be braver than they really are. As we stood outside the haunted house, I said, as casually as I could, "Todd, would you like to hold my hand while we go through there?"

"Nah."

"You sure?"

"Of course I'm sure."

"All right."

Just to be safe, I left my hand close to his. Three steps into the house, and *whap!* Both Todd's hands slapped against mine and hung on with a desperate grip.

I didn't withdraw my hand, and God won't either. His hand is always there. He'll never pull it away, you can grasp it whenever you're scared.

In Psalm 34, David revisits this theme with an additional twist: "The LORD is near to those who have a broken heart, / And saves such as have a contrite spirit."[6]

A young family in our church found this truth to be valid under one of the most horrific experiences imaginable. Their ten-month-old daughter—their firstborn—got into some furniture polish and accidentally poured it all over herself, filling her lungs with the toxic fumes.

The parents exploded into action. The father grabbed his keys, the mother picked up their child, and after quickly changing her clothes, they rushed her to the hospital. Along the way, as the mother held her precious daughter in her arms, she felt her baby go limp. Can you imagine a more frightening feeling?

Once inside the hospital, the nurses and doctors came alive with a reassuring but terrifying efficiency. The almost-lifeless child was taken from her mother's arms and rushed to an intensive care unit. And then, after such nerve-racking activity, all the parents could do was wait.

Yet, the young couple told me later, "As we sat in that waiting room with our only daughter in intensive care, we knew the Lord was with us. We could just feel His presence."

Thanks be to God, that little girl miraculously recovered. Her parents are a testimony that you never have to know hardship without also feeling God's presence. If you come to Christ, you will always have the option of an ever-present friend. You don't have to dial long-distance. He'll be with you every step of the way.

"But how?" you might be asking. "How do I feel His presence when sometimes I sense only His silence and remoteness?" That's a good question, one that all of us face—especially during bouts of fear. One psychologist said that the only two groups of people who are free from fear are the dead and the deranged, so let's spend a few moments discovering how God meets us with His presence in the midst of our fears.

■

Freedom from Fear

We all face fears, don't we? There are the "pestering" fears: Will the Thanksgiving Day dinner turn out all right? Will the client re-sign for another year? Will we be able to afford our mortgage *and* a new car this year?

And then there are the "pressing" fears, the fears that are not so easily managed or shelved. These are the fears in which our ship begins taking on water. Rumors start spreading through the company regarding massive, impending layoffs. A child begins demonstrating bizarre behavior at school. The doctor wants to take a few more tests—she sees something that worries her, and she wants to find out what it is. A spouse begins making lame excuses for increasing absences, and you start to wonder why.

Pressing fears cause mild panic. And, if we continue to worry over them, they dissipate our energy and lead us into self-destructive behavior. More than anything else, they're simply exhausting, and we just wish they would go away—but more often than not, they get worse and become "paralyzing" fears.

Paralyzing fears are the gut-wrenching, panic-producing, "I'm-going-to-die" kind of fears. I got a glimpse of this kind of fear when our church was in the early building phase of our new balcony. Somehow, I was lured by a staff member up to the uncompleted balcony to take a look at the construction. I decided to attempt a Wallenda-like walk (without a net) on a ten-inch beam for about a hundred feet over a thirty-foot drop!

I was fine on the way over, but as I started my way back, I saw the staff member who had lured me up there get scared and start to crawl on the beam! He'd probably looked down and noticed how far up he was. I was determined to show him that even if he lost his nerve, I wasn't about to lose mine. So I kept walking—but about two-thirds of the way back, I started to lose my balance.

Now, I have a pretty hard head, but in those gripping moments of absolute terror, I knew that a thirty-foot fall on concrete might be a bit much—even for a skull as thick as mine.

It was the first time I had ever felt such stark terror, and it was a very unpleasant feeling. You freeze up, your throat gets dry, your pulse races, your hands get wet, and your mind is reeling as nausea begins to take over. Thank God, I regained my composure and completed the walk. (I *kissed the ground* when I got down!) After a shower and a change of clothes, I actually felt normal again and finished my work assignments that day. But I have no intention of ever repeating that display of stupidity.

Some people experience this panic-producing fear on a regular basis. All I had to do to escape from my fear was to get down from the beam, but you might be on a precipice that feels as if it'll last forever.

My heart goes out to you. It's one thing to walk a beam over a thirty-foot drop, but it's another thing altogether when you're traveling on a lonely road through the valley of the shadow of death. What do you do then?

God's presence is with you, but you have to make a choice to believe—and I mean, really believe—that this is true. This conscious decision is yours alone. As the panic rises, you must ask yourself, *Am I going to trust in His comforting presence? Will I acknowledge His omnipresent reality? Will I allow Him to strengthen my soul? Or will I believe a lie and cry out, as so many do, "You are not near! You don't care for me, do You, God?"*

One of the main missions of God is to free us from the debilitating bonds of fear and anxiety. God's heart is broken when He sees us so demoralized and weighed down by fear.

Next time the fear rises, remind yourself, "The Lord is in this place." That's the first step. Try repeating that, over and over, until its truth begins to comfort you.

"The Lord is in this place."

"The Lord is in this place."

Next, as David urges us in Psalm 62:8, "Pour out your heart before Him." Once you've acknowledged God's presence, you don't have to pretend to feel anything different from what you're actually feeling, so tell Him exactly what is going on inside you. Weep. Moan. Even scream.

Then, call upon God. Prayer itself can defuse fear. I know that seems to defy human understanding, but I also know it's true. It works. Try it and you'll see. The Bible promises a spirit of peace that passes human understanding when we call on God. That peace—which we can't easily explain—finds a window to our spirit and begins to usher forth a welcome calm.

Finally, as you pray about a particular fear, you must learn to give God the problem that produces the fear. Don't waste all your time telling God about the problem. He already knows all about it. Instead, focus your energy on *handing the problem over to Him.*

One thing that helps me is to write out my prayers longhand. One entry might look like this: "Here and now in Your very presence I am refusing to wander in the wastelands of fear. I will not imagine worst-case scenarios, I will not make up nightmares, I will not live that way today. I am making the deliberate choice to walk in faith. As Your Word says, I will cast my cares upon You."

If doubts keep rising, go back and read Psalm 139. Ask God to make David's experience your experience. Remind yourself that God's right there and His hand is outstretched. Grab right on.

■

Stop!

I know some of you are "skimming" even as you read these words. You can't wait to get back and crank up your commerce

machine, play a round of golf, or go rent a movie. You think that the white space at the end of this chapter is your permission to "forget about God for a while" and get on with the real world. You're busy with all the pressures of the world around you, but in that busyness you're missing the most important element of all—God's ongoing presence that is available to you.

Please, just for a minute, shut everything down. Just stop. Revel in the fact that you do not have to walk alone. He's right there, all you have to do is put your hand out to Him.

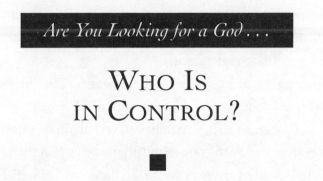

3

Are You Looking for a God . . .

WHO IS IN CONTROL?

Four hours before midnight, the commuter train lumbers into the train station. With a lurch, it jerks to a stop. Steam leaps up underneath it, the heat from its engine and brakes commingling with the cold Chicago air.

On cue, the doors slide open and a crowd of people stumble out. Many of these people jumped on the same train twelve, thirteen hours ago, looking fresh, clean shaven, neatly combed, and full of life. Now, they wander around like haggard, half-dazed, semi-humanoid creatures.

Horns honk and spouses wave as loved ones get ready to pick up the people they once viewed as the man or woman of their dreams. I notice that one man just stops and stares when he recognizes his wife's car. I get the feeling he's thinking, *Don't honk at me. Just let me walk around in oblivion for a little while.*

He begins moving, pushing his body toward the car, and finally opens the door and falls into the passenger seat.

I can picture the rest of his evening. As he walks inside his home, he throws his coat on a chair, collapses on the living room couch, and picks up the remote control. If he's a Christian, he might pray something like: "God, I hear You are an omnipotent God. I hear You are willing to flow Your cosmic, transforming energy into my life. But right now, I'll settle for a Valium and a late night rerun."

I meet a lot of people who feel "beat up" by life. Some of the people I talk to feel like victims of their circumstances. Their obligations to their families have left them trapped in a job they can barely tolerate—and that's on a good day. Others feel as if they are prisoners of their character flaws, bad habits, and addictions.

In short, many of us go through life feeling powerless. Every now and then—maybe on New Year's Day—we'll make a decision to change. We read a book on diet and exercise that pumps us up. We look at the pictures, and we dream of having a body that doesn't sag in all the wrong places. So we go out and buy a jogging outfit. While we're at the mall, we purchase a wok, because we're only going to eat vegetables from here on out. Next, we stop at the health food store and purchase a copy of *Fitness* magazine. We sign up at the health club on the way home.

Yes, siree, in two months, no one will recognize us. We'll have to buy a whole new wardrobe.

By the time Valentine's Day rolls around, we stumble across our jogging outfit—in the back of the closet. The wok, we remember, is in the garage. (We needed *something* to catch the oil leaking from the car.) The fitness magazines are buried under a month's supply of the *Chicago Tribune*. When we go to turn in our locker keys to the health club, the receptionist asks,

"Are you sure you have a membership here? I don't remember ever seeing you."

We feel so guilty we decide to stop at a fast-food restaurant on the way home and drown our feelings of defeat with a chocolate shake.

Or maybe we decide one Sunday that we're going to start controlling our anger. Maybe the pastor's sermon really spoke to our hearts, and we're determined that the angry man or woman that our kids have come to know will soon be gone forever.

We go out to the bookstore and purchase a copy of the *One Minute Manager,* and follow the guidelines to help us control of our temper at work. We put a rubber band around our wrist to remind ourselves to think positive thoughts. And we post inspirational sayings around our cubicles. At home, we use magnets to mount similar sayings on the refrigerator. For three days, we do wonderfully well, but on Thursday, just before we leave the office, our boss chews us out. We go home in a bad mood and find out that our kids have tracked mud into the house and somebody forgot to do the laundry, and within seconds we sigh in despair as that old familiar scream escapes from our throats. Our anger never died, it just took a short vacation.

Whether we are exercise wanna-bes or periodic self-improvement junkies, the scenario is always the same. Late one night, we shuffle into the kitchen, drop into a chair, put our heads in our hands, and stare blankly down at the table. "Admit it," we whisper to ourselves, "you're a weak person."

Then we lift up our heads and grimace. "I hate it," we say, "I hate being an impotent, powerless person."

Whenever I talk publicly about the unlimited power of God—God's omnipotence—I'm acutely aware of the painful

■

experiences of those who are listening. When I point out God's desire to energize each and every human life—to endow every Christian with a portion of His divine power—my words are often lost in the despair and din of unremitting defeat.

These feelings of powerlessness and hopelessness suck the energy right out of us. Instead of rejoicing when we awake with, "Oh, God, it's *good* to be alive!" we wince and groan and moan, "Oh no, how many times am I going to blow it today?" Some of us would rather stay in bed.

Throughout the day, instead of walking in the confidence that God intends for us, we limp and cower and fear the worst.

Is this you? If so, hang with me. You're about to learn one of the most energizing, encouraging, and awe-inspiring truths about God: His power is limitless and He wants to share it with *you* liberally!

■

What Kind of Power?

One day, a great leader and prophet of the Old Testament became overwhelmed with discouragement, and understandably so. Not only had he just suffered a bad day, a bad week, and a bad month, but he looked perfectly set up for a miserable life altogether. His body smelled. His hair was infested with lice. His muscles were tight and cramped from his confinement in a dank, dark, oppressive prison cell. His name had become the butt of every joke told by his countrymen, and even God seemed to be getting on his case.

As Jeremiah began to give way to self-pity, God broke through and said, "Behold, I am the LORD, the God of all flesh; is anything too difficult for Me?"[1]

Allow me to very crudely paraphrase what I believe God was saying to Jeremiah: "Hey, Jeremiah! I know that you believe in Me, but be honest. You think because you're in prison and because you're the butt of everybody's jokes, that I have lost My punch. You're in a bind, and because I haven't done anything about it yet, you assume I'm all out of power. But I'm talking to you now, Jeremiah, to remind you that nothing—*nothing*—is too difficult for Me. Got that?"

All Jeremiah needed to do was sit back and meditate on what God had already done. Think about it. What kind of power is required to speak a universe into existence? What kind of strength must someone possess to scatter stars into infinite space? How explosive do you have to be to ignite the sun or to sustain its fire? What kind of brute force is required to stack up mountains twenty thousand feet into the air?

Only one force is able to accomplish such a feat: God's power.

Throughout history, when God's people found themselves facing impossible odds, they reminded themselves of God's limitless power. Even Job took comfort by remembering "He stirs up the sea with His power . . . The thunder of His power who can understand?"[2]

Like Jeremiah and Job, we occasionally need a little reminder of what God can do, especially if things aren't going our way. In Psalm 115:3, the psalmist points out that God can do whatever He pleases. That is the essence of what omnipotence is all about. *Omnipotent* simply means "all-powerful." God never has to ask permission. His unrestrained, indescribable, infinite power and abilities have no parameters.

In fact, one time He specifically set up a confrontation between Moses and Pharaoh to demonstrate His power:

"Indeed for this purpose I have raised you [Moses] up, that I may show My power in you."[3] When God wanted to make sure Israel followed Him, what did He do? He revealed His power by breaking apart the sea. He wanted the Israelites to see exactly whom they were following and whom they were being called to submit to: "And when the Israelites saw the great power the LORD displayed against the Egyptians, the people feared the LORD and put their trust in him and in Moses his servant."[4]

Recently, some of my sailing buddies thought they had witnessed such power when my sailboat entered the Milwaukee Regatta. We had been sailing all day and the regatta was down to the final race. We had to win the last race in order to win the overall regatta. We were in third place entering the last stretch when the wind disappeared. Every boat just sat there. We waited and we waited until a fresh burst of wind came across the lake. Mouths dropped open as the other crews watched that wind hit us first. Our sails filled up and our boat passed the two in front of us, and we went on to win the whole regatta.

When I came back to the dock, most of the other boat owners gave me a hard time. They know I'm a pastor so they shouted at me, "Unfair, unfair! You have connections!"

"Well, were you praying?" I kidded them. Everybody on my boat was!

Even in fun, most people recognize that God has power over the elements—the wind, the rain, and the seas. Ecclesiastes reminds us, "No man has power over the wind to contain it."[5]

God's power is something He can dole out according to His purposes. When Israel went astray, He gave power to her enemies to punish her: "And the children of Israel again did evil in the sight of the LORD. So the LORD strengthened Eglon king of Moab against Israel, because they had done evil in the sight of the LORD."[6] God also gave this power to individuals. "And the Spirit of the LORD came mightily upon him, and he [Samson] tore the lion apart as one would have torn apart a young goat . . ."[7]

With the coming of the Holy Spirit after the death of Jesus, God's power was unleashed in even new and more startling ways. The apostles were marked by their newly found power, as recorded in Acts: "And with great power the apostles gave witness to the resurrection of the Lord Jesus."[8]

What was the source of this power? Paul explains that he and the apostles sought the "power of His resurrection."[9] Now think about that for a minute. Think about what the Resurrection accomplished for you and me. Think about all the times you felt powerless to fight off a particular sin. Yes, *that* one, the one you don't want anybody to know about. Even though you were ashamed of it, no matter how hard you tried, you kept falling and failing and blowing it.

Now, add to that sense of powerlessness the defeat you feel after every other sin you've ever committed—all the times you've let a cruel word slip out, gave vent to your temper, spoke a malicious word in gossip—add it all up. Pretty daunting, isn't it? But we're not done yet.

Multiply the power needed to overcome the sin in your own life by the numbers of all the people who ever lived. From Adam and Eve, through Homer, Plato, and Socrates, to Genghis Khan, King Arthur—all the way up through and past John F. Kennedy to the babies who are being born even as you read these words. Take *all* their sin and add it together—not just the sins they did openly, but also the secret sins that held them prisoner and that frustrated them in defeat. Don't forget to throw in the sins of Adolf Hitler and Idi Amin. And don't leave out the serial killers, drug addicts, insider traders—make sure it all gets put into the equation.

The power to break out of your sin alone seemed unlikely enough, but the thought that there could be enough spiritual power to completely obliterate the choke hold of every sin that would ever be committed by anyone who ever lived sounds beyond comprehension. Billions and billions of people were not able, even by pooling their power together, to overcome the lure of all these sins. Every person who has ever lived added to, rather than subtracted from, the pile.

Everyone, that is, except for One.

That's the power of the resurrection of Jesus Christ—a power that could overcome every spiritual failing, every sin, every weakness, in one explosive act. When Christ rose from the dead, He displayed enough raw power literally to blow apart the prison walls of hell and buy back those souls who would trust in Him. What we are powerless to do in our own lives, Christ was powerful enough to accomplish for everyone who would believe.

God's power thus extends over the physical world *and* the spiritual world. It is a power that is beyond what any of us can imagine. What's even more impressive, however, is that God is willing and anxious to share His power with us.

Strength to the Weak

I applaud God for His omnipotence. But He deserves a standing ovation for not hoarding His power. The almost-too-good-to-be-true fact is that God has made a conscious, sovereign choice to let a weak, weary, and worn-down man like me share His power.

Isaiah 40:29–31 says,

He gives power to the weak,

And to those who have no might He increases strength.

Even the youths shall faint and be weary,

And the young men shall utterly fall,

But those who wait on the LORD

Shall renew their strength;

They shall mount up with wings like eagles,

They shall run and not be weary,

They shall walk and not faint.

For years, I felt exactly what many of you might be feeling right now. It bothered me to hear people stand up and extol God's omnipotence and to keep claiming that it could have a radical effect on people's lives.

"Oh yeah?" I wanted to ask them. "Then where's the connection? I have never doubted God's omnipotence. But tell me, why are there so many spineless, weak, and beaten-down Christians? If God has the power and if He wants to channel that power into people's lives, and if we all want the power, where is the missing link?" Without sounding presumptuous, I think I've found it.

After pondering this question for the better part of twenty years, I'm ready to go public with something that I have been practicing privately for a long time. The missing link, in a word, is *faith*. Now, I know you've heard that word before, so stay with me as I explain how it can be used to translate God's power into our lives.

If you know Scripture very well at all, you know that a step of faith is often required before divine power is revealed. Consider an example from Exodus 14. After a miraculous deliverance, Moses is walking in front of a bunch of ragtag ex-slaves called the Israelites. For four hundred years, they've never been organized into an army. They don't have a single weapon among them. There aren't any military leaders either— no generals, no majors, no captains, no lieutenants—just a bunch of field hands taking a stroll toward the desert.

As the Israelites reach the outskirts of Egypt, Pharaoh realizes what he has done by letting them go. Without the Israelites, who's going to do all the dirty work? Who's going to clean the bathrooms? Who's going to make bricks in the hot sun?

Quickly, Pharaoh gathers his trained army—charioteers, skilled horsemen, and foot soldiers—all under his command and ready to bring the Israelites back into slavery. As Pharaoh's army charges, Moses looks around him and sees that he's pinned up against the Red Sea. He's got to be thinking, *Okay, God, what are You up to?*

Still following God's specific direction, Moses continues to lead Israel toward the water's edge. There's no path to escape. The people in front are getting their toes wet, and if the people in back don't stop pushing to get away from the Egyptians, things are gonna get real ugly, real fast.

Watching Moses from behind, people must have thought he had absolutely lost his mind. The first axiom of military strategy is always to give yourself an escape route. But here was Moses walking directly into the sea.

Suddenly, a power never before witnessed by human eyes unleashes itself before the startled countenances of thousands upon thousands of people. With a mighty roar, the waters begin to part and God makes a way of escape—directly across the sea bottom.

Did Moses *know* that God was going to part the Red Sea when he followed God's direction to the water's edge? I doubt it. How could he? Nothing like that had ever been done before—it was beyond human imagination for anyone to suggest that an entire nation could escape from Pharaoh by walking along a dry sea bottom.

But here's the key. Here's the missing link that translated God's power into Moses' life. *Even though Moses didn't know how God was going to intervene, he acted as though God would.* He kept walking in the direction God was leading him and just trusted that God would demonstrate His power along the way.

The same key that worked for Moses will work for you. It's worked for me.

My first real test came shortly after I received a phone call that would dramatically change my life. The upshot of the phone call could be summarized in three short, gut-wrenching words: "Dad has died."

Several days after the funeral, after watching my dad's body lowered into the ground and doing my best to comfort my grieving mother, it dawned on me that I eventually would have to face my congregation. Not only would I have to stand in front of them, but I'd actually have to deliver a sermon. I couldn't stop living just because my dad no longer walked on this earth, but if ever there was a piece of ground that I couldn't even imagine standing upon, it was the two or three square feet behind the pulpit at Willow Creek Community Church. I would rather have gone to Siberia or a snake-infested jungle— anywhere to escape the grief that I felt and the fear of getting up in front of a group of people who were waiting to hear a sermon from me.

I felt that I just couldn't do it.

After the funeral, as I returned to the Chicago suburbs from Kalamazoo, I tried to summon the strength. I worked hard to manufacture some courage—but it just wouldn't come. Nothing was there. I had absolutely no inner resources from which to draw. It seemed as though my father's death had sucked my own life right out of me. I had given everything I had in a valiant effort to comfort my mother, and now nothing was left.

This was new to me. I felt fears I had never felt before. I found myself breaking down and crying in the middle of my sermon preparation. As Saturday approached, it became very clear to me that I lacked the strength to go through with the sermon. It was one thing to be a basket case tucked away in a pastor's office. It was another thing altogether to get up in front of thousands of people and have everyone gawk at my weakness.

"I can't do it," I admitted. "I just don't have the strength."

And then a troubling thought entered my mind. *If I don't do it this Sunday, how will I do it next Sunday?* A maliciously chilling voice whispered its words of despair into my spirit: *You are not going to be able to do it, ever. You might as well get out of the ministry. You've had it. You're done!*

But then, the quiet whisper of the Holy Spirit spoke some sanity into my confused and weary mind. *Just take it a step at a time. Tomorrow morning, get up and act as though you are going to be able to preach. See if the power doesn't come. Trust Me. Show just a little faith! Walk in the direction I'm asking you to go and have faith that I will give you power along the way.*

The next morning, I woke up and, at first, I just wanted to stay in bed. Then I remembered God's gentle words. *Okay, God,* I prayed. *I'm going to get up and act as if I have the strength. I'll go as far as You allow me. If that's out the driveway, so be it. If it's to the parking lot, so be it. If it's to the pulpit, so be it. I'll move ahead, trusting that You'll give me the power I need along the way.*

My task didn't immediately become easier. I still felt a deep sadness and sense of heaviness as I showered, dressed, and drove to the church. When I finally took my place on the platform in front of the church, I wasn't overcome by a sudden burst of God's energy. And when the time came for me to stand up and walk to the podium, the battle was anything but over. As fear started to grip my throat I silently prayed, *Lord, I'm here, and I'm trusting You. I'm terribly weak this morning. But I'm going to stand up here and I'm going to act as if I'm empowered. If You empower me, fine. If You don't, I'm going to fall flat on my face . . . but here goes.*

I wish I could say that in that moment of faith I was suddenly turbocharged. But it didn't happen. A big part of my heart was still breaking, but God gave me enough power to get through that sermon. (Many people actually said they were helped by it, and I've continued to preach Sunday after Sunday since then.)

It might sound rather trivial to you, but that moment was one of the most amazing, faith-producing experiences I've ever had. It became a building block in my life upon which I have looked back many times when difficult circumstances seem to be collapsing around me. To me, preaching a sermon at that moment seemed the height of absurdity, like buying advance tickets to the Chicago Cubs play-offs. What I learned is that God has power and He's willing to share it if we step out in faith and believe that He will.

We not only need God's power to overcome our weaknesses, however. We need it to fulfill the work He's assigned to us on earth.

Power to Do Good

I was in the middle of a glorious but grueling Sunday. After preaching three weekend sermons, I prepared for a special baptismal service later in the afternoon. By the time that service was over, I had participated in the baptism of over two hundred people.

Shortly thereafter, I rushed to the airport to catch a flight to the West Coast. I was scheduled to speak at a conference early the next day.

As I boarded the plane and settled into my seat, I waited anxiously to see who would be seated next to me. I was bone weary, so I prayed, *Dear God, let it be a "reader" rather than a "talker."* Those of you who fly often know exactly what I was praying for. Some people like to carry a running commentary throughout an entire flight. Others are content to sit quietly, open a book, and maybe just nod in your direction when they finally get off the plane.

A man sat down next to me, smiled, and pulled out a book. Soon, I was smiling too. I sat back and relaxed with my own book.

To my great dismay, it soon became apparent that we weren't going anywhere. The plane sat on the ground for a full hour, during which I felt God speaking to my heart, *What if I want to be great and powerful through you?*

Lord, I responded, *I'm tired. If You need to speak to this man, You need to find someone who has more energy than I.* Immediately, the Holy Spirit's conviction gripped me, and I found myself praying a prayer of submission. *Lord, if You want to be strong in my weakness, be strong.*

Halfway through the flight (our plane eventually took off), we were served a meal, and the man seated next to me finally spoke up. "I see you're reading a book. What is it?"

Since I was reading a Christian book, his question led to a discussion of spiritual matters, and we spent the rest of the flight talking about the difference between Christianity and conventional religion. After the flight, we exchanged cards. There was no big revelation, no mile-high conversion, but a spiritual door was opened in his life.

Even though I had been engaged in a good hour or so of vigorous discussion, I felt less tired after the flight than before it. It's exhilarating to be used by God. I got off the plane and thought, *How many times did God want to be strong in me but I refused to go along?*

You see, God is great and God is powerful, but we must invite Him to be powerful in our lives. His strength is always there, but it's up to us to provide a channel through which that power can flow.

Some of you feel beat up and drained. Some of you feel like a victim who has been picked on so thoroughly that your bones are clean. Some of you face daunting tasks and stiff challenges, and you're worried that you don't have what it takes to carry on. I challenge you to act as though you are empowered, and see—just test it—if God does not send His strength your way. Determine this very moment to walk in the direction God is asking you to go and just trust that He will grant you power along the way.

Paul urges us, "Your faith should not be in the wisdom of men but in the power of God."[10] I had very little strength or wisdom with which to reach out to that man on the plane, but my inadequacy was irrelevant in the face of God's miraculous and never-flagging power.

The beauty of God's power is that it points people directly back to the source: God Himself. When Peter and John healed a lame man, and people stopped to gawk at them, the apostles were quick to remind the onlookers that the greatness they had seen was evidence of *God's* power, not their own. Peter responded: "Men of Israel, why do you marvel at this? Or why look so intently at us, as though by our own power or godliness we had made this man walk?"[11]

When people see human power revealed, they might be impressed. But the call of the gospel goes much too deep for anybody to be "impressed" into the kingdom. They have to be humbled, amazed, and awed at a power that comes from a completely different source, and only God's power, revealed in us, is up to the task.

God's power will liberate us from our weakness and equip us to do His will. It will also give us the strength to become like Christ.

Power to Be Like Christ

One day the entire drive to O'Hare Airport was an amalgam of glancing at my watch and then calculating how far I still had to drive to get there. I had meant to leave thirty minutes earlier, but I kept getting tied up, and now I stood a likely chance of missing my flight altogether.

As soon as I got to the airport, I literally ran to the ticket counter, my garment bag and briefcase in tow. Despite my rush to the airport and my urgent haste, the ticket agent displayed two infuriating speeds—slow and comatose. *Somebody ought to check this guy's pulse*, I thought. *Maybe he died and nobody knows it.*

As he moved with the deliberateness of a glacier, the thought struck me that, unlike a glacier, I didn't have two thousand years to get where I needed to go. I tapped my driver's license against the top of the counter. He didn't get the hint. Everything within me wanted to leap over that counter and say, "Resurrect yourself, man! I'm in a hurry!"

Suddenly the thought struck me, *I have a choice to make. To continue to act like an inconsiderate jerk, or to attempt to exercise self-control.* So I began wondering what would happen if I was willing to demonstrate my faith and act as a patient person would act. If I did so, would God supply the grace for me to become a patient man?

Then I paused and asked myself, *How would a patient man act in this situation?*

Well, the first thing he would do is back off the counter a little bit. So I eased back. The next thing he would probably do is put his hands in his pockets. I sunk my fists in deep. Finally, I figured a patient man might even ask the ticket agent how he's doing. I forced my mouth open.

"How has your day been?"

The guy rolled his eyes. Finally, a spark of life! "We've been really busy. And people have been yelling at me all day!"

As he ventilated his frustration he became more human to me. Suddenly, I could feel God's power transforming me into a more patient man. Even my pulse slowed down, and though the ticket agent's pulse never did pick up much, I made my flight and learned a valuable lesson (in an area that still requires lots of work in my life).

What was the key? I went ahead and performed the action, trusting God to provide power along the way. I found that faith is the bridge between God's omnipotence and our experience of His power in our lives.

Now, I almost become amused when someone says to me, "I have a friend I need to reconcile with, but I just don't have the strength." I want to say, "Reconciliation is never easy, but act as a reconciling person would act. Call that person on the phone, and see if God doesn't help you find the words to say."

Others may tell me, "I'm not a generous person." Why not begin acting like a generous person and see what God does along the way?

Are you self-centered? When those self-absorbing thoughts start flooding your mind, tell yourself, *Wait a minute. How would a selfless person act right now? I'm going to demonstrate my faith and see if God doesn't help me to act that way.*

God's omnipotence means that you can learn to change the orientation of your mind instead of collapsing into your weakness. If God can fashion the mountains, if God can keep the sun in its orbit, if God can split a sea and dry the ground beneath it so an entire nation can cross, do you doubt that He can transform your character?

I want to be candid with you, however. Changing the orientation of your mind from your weakness to God's power requires a hardball choice to trust God, a type of mental tenacity that most people don't associate with Christianity.

I face the need for God's power every single day. I'm not eloquent by nature, but almost every week I have to stand up in front of thousands of people and try to explain the Word of God to them. Almost every week my mind starts to take in fearful thoughts, such as: *This will be the time a sermon doesn't quite come together. This will be the time God doesn't use me. Here comes the big swan dive.*

I can't tell you how much energy and determination and prayer it takes for me to keep making the deliberate choice to appropriate faith and trust in the power of God.

And every time my wife and kids drive to Michigan to visit family, almost without fail, every hour and a half I think of all the calamities that can occur on the highway, and then I have to force myself to refocus on God's power to protect them.

How do I do it? I fill my mind with the truth of the identity of God. I keep an awareness of His power flowing through the front burners of my psyche, memorizing relevant Scriptures and consciously "changing the channels" of my brain until I rest in His power. I've declared war on my ignorance of God, because the challenges I face today are simply too great for me to remain in ignorance and to trust in my own resources.

The same is true of you. Get to know God. He's all-knowing. (He's omniscient.) He's always there when you need Him. (He's omnipresent.) And He's in control. (He's omnipotent.) All the "omni's" of His character have changed my life—as well as millions of lives throughout history and probably your next-door neighbor's or a friend's at work.

This is the God who will help you. This is the God who will give you the power to overcome your challenges and to fulfill the aspirations He's placed in your heart.

And even better news is that even though God is always in control it doesn't mean He is an impassive, unfeeling stoic. As we'll see in the next chapter, our omnipotent God is an expressive God, a God who is moved by the actions, feelings, and thoughts of those He has created. I can't wait to show you how even an omnipotent God is a God we can relate to.

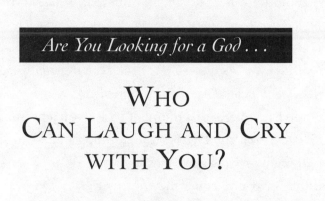

4

Are You Looking for a God . . .

WHO CAN LAUGH AND CRY WITH YOU?

"Stop laughing. You're in church. What's the matter with you?"

"This isn't the place to cry. If you can't control yourself, go to your bedroom until you get over it."

"Swallow that anger. It'll do you no good to let it out."

These voices haunted my youth. I grew up in a devout Dutch subculture in Michigan, and while that upbringing paved the way for my most precious experience—a relationship with Jesus Christ—it also gave me the impression that strong feelings of any kind needed to be "edited."

The net result was that the vibrancy of our experiences lost their definition and became bland, boring, and—even worse—patently inauthentic. As a young boy, I grew suspicious of these spiritual filters, which sucked the life out of those around me. It was as if God had created a world with succulent flavors to enjoy—curry, exotic spices, and sweet desserts—but in church we were only allowed to eat plain, white rice.

It took many years before I had the courage to question these assumptions. *Is it possible*, I wondered, *for Christ-followers to be joyful without being superficially silly? Can Christ-followers be sad and avoid the charge that they're really just morose or faithless? Can Christ-followers get angry—not just irritated, but soulfully and deeply angry—without committing a biblical infraction?*

Let me pause here for a moment to ask you a personal question: What do *you* think about the appropriateness of showing your real feelings? You may consider yourself a seeker, so what God thinks of your feelings may not matter to you just yet. But if you call yourself a Christ-follower, the question is of vital importance.

■

God Is an Expressive God

If we view God as the great philosophical stoic—impassive and unmoved by the heights of ecstasy and the depths of sadness—then we'll naturally aspire to the same character. But if God is an expressive God, holding and demonstrating a rainbow spectrum's worth of emotions, then our muted lives will be seen as an aberration, which we must grow out of rather than cultivate.

Does God Do Delight?

Does God "do" delight? If He scored a winning touchdown, would He calmly hand the ball to the referee, or would He do a celebration dance with his teammates in the end zone?

If you open your Bible to the very first chapter—the book of Genesis—you won't read far before being struck by a God

■

who delights in what He does. After each day of creation He steps back, looks at what He's done, and says, "I did well! I like what I created, and I'm delighted with the results!"

After the first five days, God performs His most stunning work—He creates human beings. Looking down upon Adam and Eve, God says to Himself, *This is very, very good.* It's so good, in fact, that God gives Himself a vacation and rests on the seventh day, delighting and basking in the glory of the created world, which sprang from His hands.

Throughout the rest of Scripture God experiences intense feelings of happiness. God shows unbridled delight when He sees people acting in ways that honor Him: when He receives worship, when He sees faith demonstrated in the most trying of circumstances, and when He sees tender love shared among His people. The God of the Bible smiles, and His heart sings with delight. "He will rejoice over you with gladness, / He will quiet you with His love, / He will rejoice over you with singing."[1]

God's unbounded joy in this passage reminds me of a good musical. I've been to enough to "feel" when a song is about to break out. The interaction builds, the characters get that look in their eyes, and you just know that somebody is going to start singing. And sure enough, somebody does.

That's the feeling in this text. God is looking over His people and He can't help but break into song. He doesn't closet Himself away in a shower, however. In full view of the angels, the evil one, or anyone who's watching, God lets out with a praise-filled chorus. He's not afraid to be known as an expressive God.

Another way to discover God's delight is to look at His earthly mirror, the person of Jesus Christ. John 5:19 says, "Whatever He [the Father] does, the Son also does in like manner." Jesus was the perfect reflection of God's nature in every situation He encountered during His time here on earth.

And it just so happens that Jesus once found Himself in one of the most expressive ceremonies that human beings will ever experience. Though today's weddings tend to be . . . well, can I be honest here? Unless you're a member of the immediate family, weddings can be about as exciting as watching a computer warm up. In Jesus' day, however, weddings were anything but boring. The ceremonies were often weeklong affairs with raucous laughter and exuberant dancing and stomach-bloating feasting and practical jokes that grew ever more elaborate as the celebration wore on. Back then, you didn't slip in a forty-five-minute ceremony between your kids' soccer games. On the contrary, you often had to wipe out an entire week to attend a wedding.

Unless, of course, you had a "reputation" to keep up, as many of the Pharisees did. The religious leaders saw Jesus' enjoyment and wondered if He liked weddings more than someone who claims to be religious should.

But that didn't stop Jesus because Jesus loved joy. He tasted delight, letting it roll off His tongue and bring dancing to His feet and laughter to His soul. In fact, one of the reasons He said we should obey Him is so that our "joy may be full."[2] (When's the last time you were commanded to have a good time?!)

The next time you look at your watch during a wedding ceremony and groan over the realization that less than five minutes have gone by since your last stifled yawn, let your mind wander back to Jesus Christ, who could bring life to any celebration—the same Person who wants to bring life to your soul this very day.

God doesn't only do delight, however. The same Jesus who rejoiced with the bride and groom is elsewhere called a "man of sorrows."

God Does Sadness

When Jesus walked up to Lazarus's tomb, He didn't put on a brave face.

He wept.

As Jesus looked upon Jerusalem and saw people wandering around and wasting their lives, He cried the bitter tears of a parent in anguish. His soul shook with sorrow, and He lamented, "They're like sheep without a shepherd. They're lost."

But nothing compared to the spirit-wrenching anguish of the night of His arrest in the Garden of Gethsemane. Sadness had never known such darkness; the ground had never before tasted such bitter tears; the air had never been pierced with more agonizing groans. Jesus, trying to explain it to His disciples, said, "My soul is exceedingly sorrowful, even to death."[3] Another version says, "My soul is crushed with horror and sadness."[4]

Jesus traveled regions of sadness that have never been trod by anyone else. He suffered through the dark valleys of betrayal. He traversed the cold mountains of desertion. And not once—*not once*—did He ever suggest that the proper response was to limit sadness, to "buck up" and paint on an artificial smile. He didn't say, "This is no way to demonstrate faith—I must get My joy back." On the contrary, He cried the pure tears of a committed, faith-filled life.

Nobody makes it through life without taking some hits. I'm not talking about glancing blows off the shoulder either. I'm talking about punches to the gut that leave you gasping for breath so intensely you wonder if you'll ever breathe again.

It's one thing for me to tell you, as I've already discussed in a previous chapter, that God knows your sorrow. But maybe it will be an additional encouragement for me to tell you that not only does God know your sorrow, He can taste its bitterness in His own mouth. I said earlier that God collects your tears in a bottle, but you also need to know that He doesn't look on that bottle with the passionless gaze of a scientist conducting an experiment. He looks on it with a rip in His heart and a catch in His throat, whispering through His tears, "Your sadness affects My soul, too, so I will honor and validate your tears by collecting each one."

When I grew up, I got the notion that if I was doing the program right—if I was being a faithful employee in CEO Christianity—I was supposed to buck up and paste a plastic smile on my face as I mastered the Christian clichés, such as "All things work for good."

That's not God's way. Lazarus's death *did* eventually work out for good, but that fact didn't dry a single one of Jesus' tears. Our anything-but-dispassionate God does sadness—deeply and thoroughly.

He also does anger.

God Does Anger

Now I'm making people nervous. Sure, we like the thought of a God who knows how to have a good time. We're comforted by the reality of a God who identifies so closely with us He can taste the salt of each tear rolling gently down our cheeks. But what hope, what encouragement, can be gained from knowing an angry God?

When we look at the mirror of God in Jesus Christ, there's no denying the fact that God gets angry. Need I remind you of the time when Jesus entered the temple and saw dishonest businessmen jacking up the prices for animals that were required as sacrifices for God? Jesus doesn't have a problem with honest business, but these guys were the moral equivalents of shop owners who start charging ten dollars a gallon for bottled water after a hurricane creates insatiable demand. They were price-gouging, they were cheating, they were turning a house of prayer into a fixed casino, and Jesus became absolutely furious.

He grabbed some ropes and tied them together to make a whip. This wasn't a flash of temper that Jesus would later regret. He knew what He was doing, He chose His actions carefully, and those actions involved using a whip to clear out the place and reclaim it for worship.

The sound of the whip cracked the air and startled the people. I can imagine the disciples stepping back, their jaws dropping to their chests, saying among themselves, "Whoa! Jesus does anger!"

I think it very likely that Jesus *used* the whip well. Money-loving men wouldn't scramble away from their cash reserves without having a good reason, and a meek, mild, and "polite" Messiah would hardly be sufficient reason. They had two choices—clear out of God's house or face His Son's wrath. (The fact that everyone there chose the former option should tell us something about what it's like to face God's anger.)

But while some of us don't even want to think about an angry God, others are caught in the trap of thinking that anger is God's *only* emotion. I know one man who grew up with the understanding: If you step one inch out of line, you get hit with the heavenly hammer. You're always just one step away from *big trouble* with God. One secret sin, and you're likely to lose your job, get evicted from your house, or contract a life-threatening disease.

This doesn't square with the biblical account of God's wrath. Psalm 103:8 says, "The LORD is . . . slow to anger." Scripture doesn't say God *never* gets angry, it says He is *slow* to get angry. God holds back His wrath as long as He possibly can unless we push Him and push Him and push Him some more. His fundamental inclination toward you and me is loving-kindness. That's the starting point. Anger is a way station to which He must travel.

How do we get God angry? Hebrews 10:26 says, "If anyone sins deliberately by rejecting the Savior . . ." (TLB). In other words, the best way to get God angry is to look at what Jesus did on the cross and say, "Big deal. Who needs that? Not my problem, not my concern, pass the remote control."

That attitude is the envelope that will carry God's righteous anger to your mailbox. If anyone deliberately rejects the Savior, that sin makes every other sin "stick" to you. And though God can be and wants to be the most loving friend and companion you could ever want, if you adopt this attitude of rejection you will find that He is the most able and fearful foe imaginable. You will have nothing to look forward to but the terrible punishment of God's awful anger, which Scripture clearly promises and fearfully describes as an anger that, in the end, "will devour the adversaries."[5]

Some of you might be inclined to slam this book shut right now. You don't want to hear this. You're angry yourself. Or you're scared. Or both. God's wrath is not a pleasant subject for people with sin problems to ponder, but we must discuss it because one thing is for sure: God's anger is always legitimate, and some of it might be directed at you!

At the same time, however, remember that God's wrath subsides in a heartbeat when a stubborn human being humbles himself and acknowledges his sinful condition. God *wants* to turn His wrath away from you, so He provided an alternative through Jesus Christ and His work on the cross. If you reject that alternative, if you even do it passively by saying, "I don't need God. I think the whole notion of my actions having any effect on God is ridiculous," then you push God to a point where He says, "All right, if you won't let Me take your sins away, then you'll have to live with them—and in them—throughout this life and into eternity."

The choice is yours. But let me remind you that when you go up against the anger of God, you are no match—you *will* get what you deserve.

Fortunately, anger is just *one* of our anything-but-dispassionate God's many emotions. Gentleness is another one.

God Does Gentleness

On one occasion I was going through some particularly difficult trials. Our church was expanding, new obligations were being put on my already sagging shoulders, and even though I knew (and had taught) about God's faithfulness and provision, in the back of my mind I wondered, *Can I possibly cope with all this? Can I adequately balance family time, devotional time, and church obligations?*

And then, after church one Sunday, a close friend took me aside and looked me in the eye. This was the type of look that lovingly demanded complete attention. "If you or your family ever have a need," he said, "I want you to know that I'll help to meet that need to the best of my ability."

As I felt the catch in my throat, I sensed a prompting in my spirit, and I prayed, *Lord, are You wrapping Your arms around me through this brother?* And the spiritual assurance that flooded my soul that instant left me with no doubt. *Yeah, You are, aren't You?*

At God's core is an intrinsic gentleness that seeks to bear our burdens. When He sees people who are feeling very fragile, as I was, He finds ways to visit them and let them know they're not alone.

God does gentleness, and He does it like no one else.

Isaiah 42:3 says, "He will not break the bruised reed, nor quench the dimly burning flame" (TLB). A hollow reed that's bending over. A wick that is barely holding on to the last vestige of its flame. Those two fragile pictures describe some of us. One wrong move—however sincere—and the reed will be finished, the flame will be snuffed out.

But God comes in, sees the most fragile of His people teetering on the brink of despair, and what does He do? He reaches out with an almost impossibly gentle touch that caresses the reed and brings new life to the dying flame. He says, "I'm going to be tender. I'm going to heal your bruises. What you need is gentleness, and I have plenty of that to give."

Yes, Jesus does gentleness. In fact few things frustrated Jesus' disciples like His gentleness. The same Man who demonstrated righteous anger as he cleared the temple utterly confounded them when He displayed an embarrassingly gentle and tender soft spot for pesky little children. It was one thing not to push them out of the way, but did He really have to stop and play with them? Did He have to hold them and welcome them onto His lap?

And what about the lepers? It was one thing to offer a drive-by greeting or healing, but Jesus had to stop and *touch* them, and, even worse, *embrace* them. At the time, leprosy was so feared that the thought of touching a leprous man or woman would make most people wretch. Leprosy ate your extremities—finger by finger, toe by toe—and turned your skin ghostly white. Leviticus 14 prescribes a severe remedy if leprosy was found in a house: The house was dismantled, brick by brick, timber by timber, and everything was taken out of the city and dumped.

Lepers themselves weren't treated much better than their houses. Though they weren't "dismantled," they were confined to the dumps and refuse pits outside the cities. When they had to enter the town, they were forced to yell out, "unclean, unclean," and people would part as they approached.

If anyone knew ostracism and blame, it was the lepers. They were the social pariahs of their day. And here was a Man who, knowing they were diseased, not only talked to them, but touched them. When Jesus wrapped His arms around these precious souls trapped in decaying bodies, it was the first embrace many of them had felt for ten, twenty, or even thirty years.

Yes, He touched them. And He healed them. He showed them a gentle side that they hadn't seen since they were babies at their mothers' breasts.

God has a gentle side that we need. Some of us need it because we've only known harshness from the "big people" in our lives. Whether it was sent hurtling our way from a parent, a boss, or even a pastor, all some of us have known is judgment, derision, chastisement, and ridicule. And God says to us, "In a relationship with Me, you'll know a kind of gentleness that will meet the need of even a bruised reed and a flickering flame."

Because God is expressive—because He does joy, sadness, anger, and gentleness—the Bible teaches that *we can personally stir those emotions in Him!*

■

Moving God

Because God allows Himself to be moved, we have the opportunity to move Him. In a way, we can make God joyful. We can bring a smile to His face by responding with openness, trust, faith, and obedience to Him. At any time throughout our day, we can think something worshipful, offer it up to God, and send a smile of delight across His eternal face.

The other side of this, of course, is that we can also break God's heart. Remember, this isn't CEO Christianity we're talking about, with an unfeeling boss and an employee's manual, with rules, rewards, punishments, and promotions. This is Christianity as God intended it—a passionate, willful, and fully emotional relationship.

In this Christianity, we don't just break a rule—we break God's heart. We don't just "step out of line"—we violate a relationship and betray a trust. We don't just "disobey"—we dishonor our closest friend. We don't just commit an infraction—we shake our fists at someone who has extended bloody, nail-punctured hands to save us.

We can arouse God's anger. We can push away Christ, become stubborn, go our own way, and move God toward anger.

And we can also elicit God's tenderness. Some of us truly need to admit, "God, I'm like a bruised reed . . . or a flickering

■

flame." If we would just honestly present our condition before God, He would meet us with tenderness.

It's sobering, it's shocking, it's almost beyond belief, but it is 100 percent biblically true: Every one of our actions and attitudes affects God. By His nature He is an expressive God and He has given us the capability of stirring His heart.

There's yet one more implication of loving an expressive God: We are rescued from an expressionless existence.

■

A Return to Vibrant Living

God's emotional photographs aren't black-and-white. They're full of colors, every one we can think of, as well as shades, hues, and blends that would boggle our imagination. When we become Christians, we are invited to join this relational, expressive, and vibrant family. God has sent His Holy Spirit to transform us into more accurate reflections of who God is, and that includes mirroring His expressiveness.

Some of us have lost the intensity of our emotions. We've edited and toned them down until we are forced to deny an essential part of what it means to be human and to be created in the image of God. God wants to restore that capacity for expressiveness. As His creatures, but even more as His children, we need to allow ourselves intense and prolonged delight without feeling guilty.

Some of us ought to enjoy nature a lot more than we do. Some of us ought to celebrate a lot more than we do. There ought to be more dancing, more parties, more laughter, more fun. Because God experiences intense joy—more intense than we could ever imagine—we should allow ourselves also to experience soul-enlarging joy.

God also invites us to express fully deep, heart-wrenching sorrow. No more false smiles. No more pretending to be "over" our grieving period when, deep in our hearts, we know we haven't even begun to grieve. No more trying to "buck up" to prove we're "spiritual." God says, "Don't run from your grief. I understand it, and you know what? I *treasure* it, keeping every single tear in a bottle. If you need to be sorrowful, be sorrowful; if you need to wail, wail away."

Some of us need to express appropriate anger. There's a lot in the world we ought to be very angry about: oppression, injustice, discrimination, and cruelty that mistreats the poor and makes fun of the disabled. God says, "Be angry. Then convert some of the energy generated by your righteous anger into transforming action."

Others of us need to experience moments of tenderness. Some of us men just don't do tender. We can't find that gear in our transmissions, so we react to situations awkwardly and inevitably find ourselves out of sync with what certain situations demand. We rob our marriages and we rob our children of an emotion that God wants us to share. It's a deadly serious thing when a man can't show tenderness to his wife and kids because he makes it more difficult for them to appreciate, understand, and know the person of God. We need to live lives that are more accurate image-bearers of our tender God.

Instead of living a black-and-white existence, we'll be released into a technicolor world of vibrancy and emotion. In doing so, we'll more accurately reflect His nature to the world around us. We'll be anything but dispassionate Christ-followers.

The God we're looking for isn't a stoic. He is anything but unidimensional. He is an expressive God who has explored depths of emotion and feelings that are beyond the realms of human understanding. This is the God we can spend an entire lifetime getting to know. This is a God who can lead us into a full and complete human existence. This is a God who feels with us. This is the God we're looking for.

5

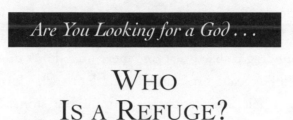

WHO
IS A REFUGE?

◼

There's one in every state, in every city, in every neigh-borhood, and in every school. A school bully is as American as baseball, democratically held elections, and church on Sunday.

You know the kind. He's twelve, maybe thirteen years old—and already shaving. Ninety percent of the male voices in your school resemble the cherubic pitches of a boys' choir, but this lug's voice sounds like a foghorn.

Our school bully was named Phil. I'm not sure what twelve-year-old terrorists grow up to become, but from watch-ing Phil in gym class, our antihero had all the makings of a sumo wrestler.

One of my closest friends, Don, casually made the brilliant, but potentially lethal, observation that, when walking out of the shower, Phil resembled one of the characters in a popular movie series at the time: *The Planet of the Apes*. The resemblance was uncanny, once you thought about it, and word of Don's astute

◼

observation brought howls of appreciation from our fellow classmates—until it reached the ears of Phil.

Words weren't exactly Phil's favorite mode of communication. He much preferred fists, and one day after school Phil found Don. All of us, including Don, knew the fight was inevitable. Yet even the hardest of hearts watching this one-sided pounding realized that one mere joke didn't deserve this.

As Phil's meaty fist crashed into Don's cheek, nose, and forehead, I felt a sickening nausea fill my stomach, and I thought, *Can't somebody stop this?* After a while, Phil grew tired of adding several new and vivid colors to Don's face, and he let him go. A friend and I helped pick Don up and commiserated with him as we walked home, all of us agreeing that it's probably not a good idea to make fun of a twelve year old who shaves.

Unfortunately, Phil's memory was as long as his IQ was low, and for the rest of the semester, until someone else raised Phil's ire, Don found himself in a desperate pursuit of refuge whenever Phil was in an obviously bad mood.

Maybe you've never been in Don's sweat-soaked shoes. Maybe you've never felt the stark terror of hearing your name called by a sneering voice. But you've probably experienced a nightmare in which you were being chased. Your lungs are burning, your legs are rebelling, but fear is driving you on. The faster you run, the closer the footsteps behind you come, until finally, mercifully, you wake up.

In ancient Middle Eastern culture, a good share of running and chasing also went on—only it was for real. Populations were spread out and judicial systems were few and far between. People kept law and order though a rudimentary form of tribal crime and punishment. If someone in your family was killed, your relatives would call a meeting and somebody would be appointed as a "blood avenger."

The task was as gruesome as its name. A blood avenger was a representative from the family whose full-time job was to find the murderer and release his or her neck from the burden of having to carry a head.

Now, when your family sat down to choose a blood avenger, you didn't choose rotund Aunt Ethel. You chose someone like fleet-footed Cousin Nick. Nick would then track down the whereabouts of the person who murdered your relative, and wait for him to go out into the field. Then, when the opportune moment arrived, Nick would step out of the bushes, announce that he was your family member's blood avenger, and the chase was on.

As a matter of honor, the blood avenger would chase the killer until only one of them was standing. Either the killer was himself killed, or the blood avenger ran completely out of breath and was physically unable to continue. Yet after a rest period the blood avenger would begin again. Final justice demanded that the family eventually receive proof of the kill, and then a celebration was in order.

Admittedly, it was more than a little crude, but it kept law and order. The major problem with such a system, however, was the mitigating circumstance of an accidental homicide.

Let's say a woman is in a hurry to go to the market. She jumps on her camel and takes off. A five year old steps out in front of her. She tries to stop. She screams out a warning and pulls on the reins with all her might, but the child is trampled. Horrified, the woman jumps down and tends to the little one as best she can, but it's too late. He dies.

Now what happens? The five year old's family calls a meeting, and they appoint a blood avenger whose orders are clear: "Track down that housewife and catch her out in the open when her back is turned. Chase her until she can't run another step, then kill her."

I bet you want to say, "That's not fair. She didn't mean to kill the little boy. It was an accident."

You're right, of course. Justice lacked a certain amount of sophistication in those days. But nobody knew what else to do. No one, that is, except God. In the Old Testament books of Deuteronomy, Numbers, and Joshua, God addresses the problem by establishing "cities of refuge":

> Speak to the children of Israel, saying: "Appoint for yourselves cities of refuge, of which I spoke to you through Moses, that the slayer who kills a person accidentally or unintentionally may flee there; and they shall be your refuge from the avenger of blood."[1]

The Israelites did as God suggested. They chose six cities for their geographical location and easy access. Throughout Israel they put up signposts pointing the way. If someone committed an accidental homicide, he would take off running to the nearest city of refuge. Once inside the city gates, he was safe from the blood avenger's wrath. The city acted as a voluntary prison to hold the suspect until a fair trial could take place. If during the trial that person was found guilty of intentional murder, he was handed over to the blood avenger. If it was found that the death was an accident, the local officials sent the blood avenger back home.

These cities of refuge flow right out of the very heart of God, and they paint a beautiful picture of God's concern for us. Bound up in the nature and character of God is the desire to provide safety and refuge to people who are feeling hunted down and oppressed.

■

Hide Here for a Time

One of the most beautiful pictures of spiritual refuge is found in Psalm 91:4:"He will shield you with his wings!" (TLB). Have you ever seen little chicks hop around, chirping, pecking, doing "chick stuff"? If the mother hen becomes aware of a predator, she doesn't schedule a seminar, plan a self-help class, or start handing out audiocassettes. She lifts her wings and, within seconds, all the baby chicks disappear underneath them.

Where once there was a doting hen and several perky side-kicks, now the predator sees nothing but one mean-looking mama who just dares the enemy to take a step forward. And in the blackness under her wings, her chicks are saying to one another, "Did you see the teeth on that wolf?"

Eventually, the chicks will have to crawl out and face the real world. But for a season, there is nothing quite like the soft shelter of those wings—the downy feathers caressing their heads; the mother's warmth stilling their shakes; her heart's steady beating gradually calming their fears.

Today, God delights in spreading His protective wings and enfolding His frightened, weary, beaten-down, worn-out children. "Hide here for a time," He says. "Get out of the danger. Regroup. Recuperate. Find new strength."

Of course, the time will come when God will gently lift His wings and urge His children to venture back out into their world, but they will do so a little calmer, a little stronger, and a little more secure.

■

While this might be the best news some of you have ever heard, others may be saying to yourself, "God is my refuge? Big deal. I don't need a city of refuge at the moment. Everything's fine."

Who Needs It?

For 99 percent of the Israelites, cities of refuge didn't mean very much. Sure, the people knew they were there if they needed them, but most of them rarely did. However, to that housewife who accidentally killed the five year old on the way to the market, the closest city of refuge was the most important place on the planet. Disneyland, Paris, Venice, Palm Beach— none of them held the allure, urgency, or call of Kedesh, Golan, Shechem, Hebron, and the other cities of refuge.

Just imagine the innocent woman as she literally runs for her life. She looks over her shoulder, the blood avenger gaining. She gauges her distance to the city gates of Kedesh, and pleads with her legs not to give out on her just yet. She hears the avenger's footsteps drawing ever closer. Soon, she even hears the man's heavy breathing. Perhaps she feels an errant swipe that just barely misses the back of her neck.

And then, with a desperate lunge, she falls through the gates and the blood avenger pulls up short. She looks at his maniacal eyes, he looks at her terrified countenance, and she holds her breath until he turns his back, at which point the woman cries out, "Yea, God! I'm safe!"

Who needs a city of refuge? Oppressed people. Weary people. Fearful people. Grieving people. Worried people. Disappointed people. Lonely people. Heartbroken people. People who are being unfairly attacked. Psalm 9:9 promises, "The

LORD also will be a refuge for the oppressed, / A refuge in times of trouble."

If someone is "hearing footsteps" draw ever closer, God swings open His magnificent gates and calls out, "Come on in." He delights in providing a refuge. Doing so isn't an avocation for Him. It's not a side job or hobby that occupies His evening hours. On the contrary, it's the heart of what He does and the essence of what it means for Him to be our God. His overwhelming, irrational love for us makes it a joy for Him to hide us for a time.

In the short run, maybe everything is going quite nicely for you. But can I suggest something that I've gleaned from spending over two decades in the ministry? If you think your entire life will be smooth sailing, you're wrong. The odds are overwhelming that between this day and the day you die you, like every one of us, will have more than your share of heartache, pain, and adversity. At that moment, you'll understand your need for a safe harbor.

Safe Harbors

In junior high, my father and I sailed out of South Haven Harbor on the Michigan side of Lake Michigan for an afternoon on the water. After about an hour my father got a mischievous look in his eye.

"What do you say we sail all night over to Chicago, just you and me?" he asked. Chicago was about seventy miles away, and sailing there sounded like the most fun a boy in junior high could possibly have.

With new energy and enthusiasm, we set our sails for Chicago and settled in for an all-night trip. About halfway across Lake Michigan, however, we were hit by a fierce storm.

I had seen plenty of storms before, but this one had an attitude. The wind howled as the waves started breaking over the boat, and I knew we were really in trouble when my dad came back and tied a rope around me.

"What's this for?" I asked.

"I'm tying you to the boat," he said, completing the knot around me, then tying the other end of the rope to a cleat.

We made some sail adjustments and I stayed in the cockpit, watching the driving wind and rain pelt and assault our boat. We stayed up all night, fighting the waves, trying to read the wind, trimming our sails, and working furiously to maintain our course.

As morning drew near, we could finally see the lights of Chicago, and strength poured into our tired limbs as we continued battling the waves and working to get our boat inside the breakwater. This storm not only had an attitude, it had staying power.

Finally, we reached the outer piers and passed into the harbor. Once we tied up on the dock I looked back over my shoulder at the open water, and for the first time in my life I had a vivid understanding of how wonderful a protected harbor can be. Three hundred yards away, a storm was spewing its bile on every boat trying to navigate Lake Michigan's waters. But in this protected bay we found refuge, a hiding place from the storm.

We felt safe, we felt protected, we felt secure. The storm couldn't touch us here. We were able to recuperate, get reorganized, fix a few things that had broken, and regather our wits about us, knowing that later on we would have to begin our return sail to South Haven.

When adversity hits, there comes a time when Scripture tells us to find a refuge fast. We can solve other problems later. Our immediate need is to get out of the storm.

Scripture says that God is that refuge.

Well, if God offers Himself as a refuge, where are the gates? How do we enter this city?

■

Entering the City of Refuge

The first step of accessing the refuge that God provides sounds so remarkably simple that many of you will miss its brilliance.

Call on God

To enter God's refuge, we must first call out to God. Psalm 91:15 says, "He shall call upon Me, and I will answer him; / I will be with him in trouble; / I will deliver him and honor him."

For the life of me, I can't figure out how this calling-on-God thing works, but it does. The Bible tells us to walk by faith, not by sight, and this is one of those times when we can't understand why something works, we can only trust in God and then be delighted when we experience it.

For centuries now, Christians have poured out their hearts to the Lord and found treasured moments of refuge. This is incredibly good news. We don't have to get out a map, calculate how far away each one of the cities of refuge is, and then embark on a journey. We don't have to drive to a monastery. We don't have to call a minister. We don't have to wait until the next church service. The front seat of our cars will work nicely. Our offices, our homes, our construction trailers—they're all as

■

good as the most elaborate cathedral. We can access the refuge of God anytime, anywhere. All we have to do is to acknowledge our need, move from self-sufficiency to dependence, and ask God to become our hiding place.

I remember several years after my dad died getting a call from my brother. "Hold on to your seat, Bill, but we just found out that there's a strong possibility that Mom has cancer."

"You've got to be kidding!" I said. But he wasn't. I drove back to Kalamazoo as quickly as possible. After an operation, we learned that Mom's tumor was malignant.

Five kids gathered around the bed of a one-hundred-pound, four-foot-eleven lady. We were stunned, somewhat disbelieving, and heartbroken. None of us wanted our mother to go through this and none of us wanted to face the reality that we might soon be left without either parent.

It all happened so fast. I had been traveling on cruise control for weeks, even months. Sure, there had been irritations. There had been problems, with a little *p*, but nothing that cried out for a place to hide, nothing that made me feel I needed to find a place of refuge.

The fear of losing my last surviving parent carried a new intensity for me. Now, all of a sudden, I needed a refuge. I needed a God who could "hide me away" and help me face my fears.

I cried out, and He was there. He opened the gates of His city and I entered right in. For a time I felt God's enfolding protection and care. (Fortunately her tumor was removed in time and she made a full recovery.) I don't understand it, but my experience meshes with the experiences of millions of Christians across the world and throughout the centuries. If we simply cry out to God in our need, He responds and becomes a refuge for us.

Pour Out Your Concerns

The next step to entering God's refuge is to pour out whatever is vexing us. Psalm 62:8 says, "Pour out your heart before Him; / God is a refuge for us." In a curious way, the passwords that open the gates into the refuge of God are the soul-wrenching words that flow out of our hearts when we finally decide to trust God. It happens when we tell Him how bad it really is and how close to the edge we really are. Somewhere in the middle of taking that step of faith, the gates open, and God's wings extend.

One of the people who had to learn this lesson was Jeremiah, an Old Testament prophet. God called Jeremiah to speak truth into a hostile environment. This was *not* a fun job. It wasn't sharing your faith on the beaches of Hawaii. This was the "go minister to the Islamic fundamentalists in the Middle East" kind of assignment, which upon receiving you ask, "Are You sure, God?"

Imagine if you were a referee at a professional football game and on the last play you had to tell the hometown crowd that the last-second, game-winning touchdown was being called back on a penalty. You'd probably want to borrow one of the player's helmets, wouldn't you? That's the situation Jeremiah faced when he spoke God's message. People just didn't want to hear what God wanted to say through him. They tried to shout Jeremiah down, and when that didn't shut him up, they beat him and put him in a set of stocks in front of the public gate of the city. Thus humiliated, Jeremiah was forced to stand by while the cruel lowlifes of his day came out to taunt him and make jokes at his expense.

Jeremiah felt so worn down by all this resistance and hostility that he finally lamented, "I have become a laughingstock all day long; / Everyone mocks me . . . / Because for me the word of the LORD has resulted / In reproach and derision all day long."[2] Then he gets morose. "Cursed be the day when I was born; / Let the day not be blessed when my mother bore me! / Cursed be the man who brought the news / To my father, saying / 'A baby boy has been born to you!' "[3]

When you're speaking words like these, you're about as low as you can get. Jeremiah is saying, "I hate my birthday. I even hate the guy who passed out the cigars announcing my birth!"

And yet, look what happens in the middle of this chaotic, unedited prayer. Jeremiah stops and says, "But the LORD is with me like a dread champion . . . / Sing to the LORD, praise the LORD! / For He has delivered the soul of the needy one / From the hand of evildoers."[4]

This prayer shows that Jeremiah is regrouping. "Wait a minute. I'm still alive. And somehow, mysteriously, I still feel cared for in this moment."

Weakness is your friend here. Nothing will extinguish your experience of God's love like false piety and dishonest heroism. Give it up. Pour out your heart to God and tell Him how you feel. Be real, be honest, and when you get it all out, you'll start to feel the gradual covering of God's comforting presence. The footsteps behind you may not cease, but they'll grow dimmer. The opposition will feel less intense. Your legs and spirit will feel a little stronger. The sky will seem a little lighter.

You may not know *how* God will come through, but somehow, you know He *will*. The actual way of escape might remain a mystery, but there will be no doubt about who will create it— your constant, caring companion, your God.

If you have never been hidden away under God's wings, you don't know what you're missing. And the best part about this is that God says it's okay to stay there for a time. I don't think He is in any particular hurry to push us out into the world again. In extreme cases of distress, I think God would even advise us to orient our lives, our schedules, and our activities around safe times with Him. In such times, our agenda should probably include safe friends and long periods of uninterrupted moments in safe places until we heal and regroup and gain enough strength to make an entry back into real life.

If you are looking for permission for this kind of "time-out," look no farther than the life of Jesus. Nobody before or since has faced the responsibilities, duties, and pressures that Jesus bore, yet sometimes He would take an entire day and an entire night, grab a couple of disciples, and retreat to a safe place—a boat, the far side of a mountain, a secluded spot in the desert. And there, Jesus would enter the refuge that His Father had prepared for Him. Surrounded by safe people, Jesus could pour out His troubles to a God who would hear the passwords and cover Him with His wings.

In that place of shelter, Jesus could regroup, restore His strength and sense of purpose, and get ready to go back into the world, working with all His might to claim it for the Father's love.

I've got even better news for you. Though the city of God's refuge is an incredible experience on earth, God has something even better in mind.

■

The Final City of Refuge

The Bible teaches that there is an eternal city of refuge that awaits all of us who are His children. In this city, called heaven, you will never hear another footstep chasing you. No twelve-year-old terrorist named Phil will live there. No blood avenger can ever get through the gate.

Even the internal demons—heartbreak, loneliness, hurt, misunderstandings, frustration—won't make it through the city limits. The damage done to us on this earth will never find its way into that safe city. We can relax, we can rest, and though some of us can hardly imagine it, we can prepare to feel safe and secure for all of eternity. Never a threat, never a worry, never a fear. All of that will be gone.

This final city of refuge is open to any and to all who would choose to enter it through the person of Jesus Christ. And right now, even if you feel unworthy, I want to ask you to consider trusting Christ and entering in. Come under His wings, hide out with God for a time, and let Him explain in greater detail His eternal city of refuge where you will be safe and secure forever.

This is the place that you know you've needed to visit. This is the Protector you've always wanted. This is the truth that can give you the strength, courage, and commitment to face another day. This God of refuge is the God who will save you from the Phils of this world, from the blood avengers, and from those who threaten to suck the life right out of you.

Even more than that, this is the God you're really looking for.

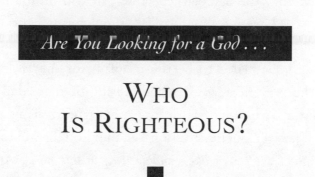

6

Are You Looking for a God . . .

WHO
IS RIGHTEOUS?

It was a glorious Saturday. Our park district touch-football team had just faced our toughest opponent of the season—and we had put them away! We were muddy and we had a few new bruises and a few sore muscles that would remind us of our middle-aged exertion over the next few days. But as guys picked up their shirts, removed their knee braces, and exchanged high fives all around, the testosterone flowed and the fellowship oozed and we felt great. It was a wonderful start to the weekend.

And then came Sunday.

Church went fine, but that afternoon, I decided to watch the Chicago Bears, and my weekend went "south" rapidly. The Bears allowed themselves to be thoroughly embarrassed on nationwide television by the Seattle Seahawks. Seattle is a beautiful city, but that year they had an ugly football team. Even so, Chicago made them look like a Super Bowl contender.

After a running back had dropped the team's tenth screen pass, I slammed my foot down and yelled at the television, "I could do better than that!" I remembered my park district team's victory the day before. "How can you drop a five-yard screen pass? Give me a uniform! I'll show you what to do with the ball!"

Well, I happened to be the chaplain for the Bears at the time. The very next week, while visiting their headquarters, I rounded a corner and ran into a mountain wearing a Bears' practice jersey. Looking eye to navel, the thought went through my mind, *I don't even like standing next to this navel.* And then another thought occurred to me: *What would it be like to crouch in front of the owner of this navel, forced to maintain a three-point stance, and hear him growl, "All right, Hybels, I'm going to eat you for breakfast"?*

I remembered my comments on the previous Sunday— "Give me a uniform. I could do better than that!"—and I realized that most of these guys could ruin me without breaking a sweat.

Just then, another player came up behind me and put an arm around my shoulder. It felt as if a tree trunk had collapsed on top of me. "How ya doin', Bill?"

"Fine, until you dislocated my shoulder."

In an instant, reality cut into me with a vengeance. With the taste of a touch-football victory fresh in my mouth, I had begun to fancy myself as having NFL potential. When I stepped inside the Bears' locker room, I was jolted back to the truth. I doubt their equipment manager could even find a pair of shoulder pads to fit me!

As a pastor, I frequently hear people make the same mistake with God and His righteousness. They'll say, "I admit, I've sinned a few times. Yeah, I've slipped. I haven't lived up to my moral potential, but I'm sure I'll hold my own with the competition. I'm sure I'll grade out in the middle of the pack somewhere."

We compare ourselves to Chicago politicians, rapists, and murderers, and reason that we look holy in comparison, but when we do that, we're using the wrong yardstick. We don't have a clue about how holy, how righteous, and how impossibly high God's standard is. When we walk into the blazing presence of God, my experience of walking into the Bears' locker room will be magnified a million times. We'll realize our holiness worked fine in the church leagues, but it can't come close to making it in heaven!

Righteousness—true, God-birthed, God-breathed, God-given righteousness—is completely misunderstood by our culture today. Of all the things we lack about God and His identity, this may be the worst ignorance on our part.

■

Our Righteous God

So many passages in the Bible call God righteous, you could almost do biblical roulette and wind up with one. Let me cycle through three:

■ "For the LORD is righteous, / He loves righteousness; / His countenance beholds the upright."[1]

In short, the psalmist says, God is not a crooked county judge. He accepts no manila envelopes and He has ordinary-sized pockets. He not only *is* righteous but He *loves* righteousness. You'll never get Him to turn the other way.

■ "Righteous are You, O LORD, / And upright are Your judgments."[2]

■

God has intrinsic righteousness. Righteousness not only defines God, but God defines righteousness. He Himself is the standard. All His laws are righteous laws; there isn't a single one that is unfair or unrighteous.

■ "His righteousness endures forever."[3]

God is not on a righteous roll for a season. He doesn't have righteous days and unrighteous days. His righteousness will endure forever.

Every decision God makes is a good and right decision, so we can be certain that every decision God makes regarding us will be a right one. We may not like the judgment, but we will never be able to quarrel with its rightness.

Furthermore, every single law that God has spoken into existence is a righteous law. God isn't swayed by the color of our skin, the size of our office, or the amount of our tithe check. His laws are "equal opportunity" and apply across the board. There is no discrimination, and no affirmative action either—just all-around, perfect righteousness. Every law protects us from harming ourselves, from harming or being harmed by others, or from squandering our lives and eternities. Each one emanates from an inherently righteous core and applies the same standard regardless of our gender, our age, our religious affiliation, or our heritage.

It's because of the inherent righteousness of God that we have developed our acute sense of fair play. Even little kids take flagrant offense at the smallest sign of unfair play. The world has yet to see a parent of more than one child who isn't bitterly accused with the words, "But that's not fair!" Although the same charge has been leveled at God, it's a ridiculous one. In fact, it's stunning just how fair God really is.

In His nature, in His actions toward us, in His laws, and in His history, God has proven Himself to be a righteous God. This righteousness has the potential to completely revolutionize our world.

■

A Righteous Revolution

Recently, my travels took me to downtown New York City. Roaming the streets, I thought I had woken up on a distant planet.

In Chicago, if you want to go to a retail store, you walk in and you shop and then you walk out. In the section of New York where I was shopping, you walk up to the door, you push a buzzer, and an armed guard checks you out to see if he's going to let you in.

You walk around the shop, acutely aware that less than ten feet away is a man with a loaded gun making sure you stay on your best behavior. When you get back out onto the sidewalk, your ears flinch from the wail of yet another siren. Your eyes are saddened by the sight of homeless people who shuffle and mumble along the streets with an aimless futility. Wrecked cars clutter the side of many streets. And the fact dawns on you, New York City is not the righteousness capital of the world.

As I sat in a New York restaurant late at night, another thought hit me: *What if there were a righteousness revolution in New York City?* It was late at night, I was away from home, so I had some time to play with the thought for a little while. What if this revolution was extended a little farther. What if there was a righteousness revolution in Chicago? Or in L.A.?

What would it be like to live in a righteous city or a righteous nation or a righteous world? No corruption in govern-

■

ment—no payoffs, no pork barreling. No crime, no violence. Women could walk the streets at midnight and feel as safe as they would at noon. There would be no locks on doors (no lost car keys!), no abuse, no murder, no theft.

I took this even farther: What would it be like to live in a righteous family? Then I really got imaginative: What would it be like to be a member of a righteous church? No one honking impatiently in the parking lot. The choir would sing on pitch and the sermon would always end on time!

If you're saying to yourself, "Interesting, but I'm afraid life would get a little boring," I beg to disagree. Because righteousness is such a foreign concept to us, we can barely relate to how much fun it would be to live in a righteous world. Christianity says we were created by a righteous God to flourish and be exhilarated in a righteous environment. In other words, God has "wired" us in such a way that the more righteous we are, the more we'll actually enjoy life.

Check my thinking on this. I went golfing with a guy some months ago. (He dragged me out there, really!) He lined up right, gripped the club right, and hit the ball right. I lined up wrong, held the club wrong, and hit the ball onto the wrong fairway. By the fourth hole, I was frustrated. By the sixth hole, I loathed the game. By the ninth hole, I was strongly considering driving the golf cart into the lake to put an end to this misery. Yet as I looked over at my partner, it was clear that he was having the time of his life.

What made the difference? He was playing the same game I was, but he was playing it rightly—and enjoying it accordingly. I was playing it wrongly, and hating every minute of it.

What makes competition so much fun is when everything seems to go right—something I rarely experience when I play golf, but which I have occasionally experienced when I'm on a sailboat.

Doing Things Rightly

As you may have guessed, my favorite sport is sailboat racing. During the summer of 1994, my team's boat made it to the final of five races in a key regatta. Everything came down to this one last race. If we won it, our boat would win the entire regatta. If we lost it, well . . .

Before the race began, I gave my crew a little pep talk to make sure that wouldn't happen. "Guys," I said, "if we ever did things right, let's do them right now."

Heads nodded and we began mapping out our strategy. This wasn't the time to guess or to "hope" that things would turn out our way. We knew how to sail. We knew our boat. We knew the lake. And this was the time to sail the way we knew how to sail, leaving nothing to chance.

We got everything all figured out, and we went for it. We started rightly. We tacked away and were just where we wanted to be on the course. We read the wind shifts rightly. We did our spinnaker hoists and drops rightly. We called the tactics rightly. *And we won*. For about two and a half hours, I experienced the exhilarating heights of doing things the right way.

We went back to the club and the guys on the other boats in our class came up to us and said, "You put on a clinic today! It was an honor to watch you sail like that—it was all done just right."

But we were only able to maintain "rightness" for a short, two-and-a-half-hour period. The longer we compete, the less

■

likely it is that we're going to do everything right. But we'll never have as much fun and true enjoyment as when we do everything just as it's supposed to be done.

God's laws will produce a society and a character that ultimately all of us want to have produced. If we let God have His way in our lives, people eventually will come up to us and say, "You put on a clinic today. It was an honor to watch you live like that—it was all done rightly." And they will mean it.

That's why David says, "I will delight myself in Your commandments, / Which I love."[4]

Will you let a righteous revolution start with you? Are you willing to serve as the "infecting agent" of righteousness? It may not be as hard as you think. We've got a role model: our righteous God.

God's righteousness is the basis on which our own sense of righteousness is born. We hinted at this in the first chapter when we talked about a universal moral code.

Outrage

Why are we sickened when we hear of men who beat their wives? Why are we outraged when we hear of children who are molested? Why are we so furious when we hear of someone preying on the elderly and cheating them out of their savings? Why? Because God has placed a moral code in our souls.

When I was in New York, I saw a doorman grab hold of an elderly woman. Her tattered clothing, unkempt hair, and weather-beaten face screamed "homeless." It was hard to see what kind of threat she could be. In the eyes of the doorman, she was certainly a nuisance, but just as certainly not a threat. Yet the doorman pushed her so hard she almost fell over.

"This is the last time I want to see you here," he yelled, and nobody watching would have doubted the doorman's serious intentions.

I thought to myself, *Long ago, this woman was someone's little girl. Maybe she's someone's mom, even someone's grandma. Here's a woman in the twilight years of her life, who matters to God, and she is getting pushed out into the cold.* And I thought, *This is so wrong. This is so very wrong.*

If I felt that way, you can imagine what goes on in the mind and heart of an intrinsically righteous God.

During that same New York trip I spoke with a Christian leader on the East Coast. He pulled me off to the side and said, "I just need a couple of minutes with you. Someone in our church sexually molested my daughter."

I was so filled with outrage I could barely contain myself. Even so, my reaction paled in comparison to what must take place in the heart of a righteous God who is intrinsically sickened with such wickedness.

Because God is righteous, He does not look on unrighteousness dispassionately. He hates it. You cannot believe how badly God wants to bring about a righteousness revolution in this world. He wants to set it all right—everyone and everything. He wants this because He loves us, and He knows that we were made to live righteously.

Even so, God is not a pirate. He's not going to step in and steal our free will. He will not overwhelm us. He will not grab control of our lives and rewire us for "autopilot."

Instead, He grieves as we lie to ourselves in a vain attempt to explain away our unrighteousness. We use projection: "It's not really my fault, it's someone else's." "Eve gave me the fruit—what was I supposed to do?" We use rationalization: "I have to go 65 in a 55 mph zone. With all these truckers, I need to go with the flow to protect my wife and children." We use comparisons: "If you think I drink a lot, you ought to spend an evening with Frank." We use suppression, pushing the guilt out of our mind as quickly as it enters. We use distraction, filling our lives with noise and busyness to avoid any time for contemplation. We use escapism—a pill, a drink, a hit, a gamble, anything to keep the adrenaline flowing.

None of these work very well. All of them eventually break down and leave us exhausted, defeated, and feeling miserable. (In other words, they leave me feeling as though I just played a round of golf!)

Into this world, God wants to launch a righteousness revolution, one that will be born in the hearts of His people. What will such a revolution require? The first step is to reestablish God's righteous standards.

Start Looking Up!

According to Boston College professor William Kilpatrick, the Western world was fairly clear on the standards of morality and virtue for about eighteen centuries. In his book, *Why Johnny Doesn't Know Right from Wrong,* Dr. Kilpatrick says that when people wanted to know what was right and what was wrong, they looked *up*. They agreed that God is a righteous God and that His righteous laws ought to rule our conduct.

Certainly, that consensus didn't guarantee compliance. It didn't mean there weren't people who did their best to break every law possible. But people still accepted the fact that transcendent, righteous laws existed and that these laws had God as their author. And most people also believed society would work better if those laws were respected rather than rejected.

About the middle of the eighteenth century, Kilpatrick notes, some alternative theories arose. The philosopher Immanuel Kant gave birth to *rationalism* by arguing, "If you want to know the difference between right and wrong, you don't have to look up because we are smart. You need only to use pure human reason. If you sit down and think, if you contemplate it, meditate on it, and incubate the problem in your mind, you will be able to figure out what is right and wrong for you."[5]

Next came the Swiss philosopher, Jean-Jacques Rousseau. Whereas Kant said, "Look to your mind," Rousseau said, "Look to your heart." That's *romanticism*. He saw the human heart as a beautiful, unfolding flower and believed that people are naturally good and will get even better if they follow the pull of their hearts, so he urged people at a moral crossroads to do whatever their hearts led them to do.

Finally, along came Friedrich Nietzsche. Nietzsche said, "Don't look up, look to your will. Just take power. Take control of your life. Decide what you want to do, how you want to manifest your energy, and do it."[6] With apologies to Nike ("Just Do It"), the disaster of Nietzsche's approach was made most apparent when a young German politician named Adolf Hitler acted on this type of thinking. Hitler's will dictated that it was wrong for Jews to live, and he acted accordingly.

Ironically, historians call the 150-year reign of the philosophies of Kant, Rousseau, and Nietzsche the "Enlightenment." Kilpatrick calls the time since that period (which ended in the middle of this century) the "Darkening." He uses this label to refer to the darkening of the human soul, citing all the staggering and depressing statistics that you and I know so well—soaring divorce, crime, suicide, and the like. According to Kilpatrick, unless we stop making gods of our minds, our hearts, and our wills, and instead use all three to look up—unless, that is, we reestablish God's righteous standards as the ultimate test of what is truly right and truly wrong—*we are doomed*.[7]

Looking inward hasn't made us a more righteous world, and unrighteousness clearly hasn't made us a happier people. The fact is, the righteousness of God has withstood Kant and Rousseau and Nietzsche and everybody else. It's clear that a righteousness revolution won't be birthed from a new philosophy. Instead, individuals are going to have to be liberated one at a time from the enslaving power of unrighteousness.

Breaking the Chains of Unrighteousness

I began meeting with a young man a number of years ago. He was a spiritual seeker and we spent several sessions working through the existence of God, the reasons for faith, and all the things he said were keeping him from becoming a Christ-follower. After several months I realized that there wasn't a single argument that would convince this young man to become a Christian. We agreed that there really wasn't any point in continuing our discussions. I didn't think I'd ever see him again.

A few years later, this young man greeted me after a Sunday service. He shook my hand with an uncharacteristic energy, and told me about his acceptance of Christ. Of course, I was surprised since he had been so closed, but my young friend explained, "When we met, all your points made perfect sense, but I was living with my girlfriend at the time, and I knew that if I became a Christian I'd have to stop sleeping with her. The bottom line was, I didn't want to stop—and there was nothing you could have said to overcome that objection."

This young man knew Christianity was true. He knew Christianity was right. He accepted the fact that God had a righteous claim on his allegiance, but his slavery to unrighteousness kept him from doing what he really wanted to do. Intellectual arguments were just a subterfuge to protect his immoral choices.

Romans 6:17–18 teaches, "Thanks be to God that, though you used to be slaves to sin, . . . you have been set free from sin and have become slaves to righteousness"(NIV). In the day in which this text was written, slavery was rampant, so the apostle Paul uses that imagery to make his point. He's saying, "Everybody's a slave—either to God or to his sin. Don't kid yourself. You are addicted to unrighteousness and you can't break out of it by your own strength."

Have you ever been to a fair where they were giving hot-air balloon rides? The balloon is inflated through the heat of a burner, but the balloon doesn't go very far up into the sky because it is tethered to a stake. We are all tethered to the stake of our sin. Until that rope is cut by a power outside ourselves, we will not ascend very high. We may agree with God's righteous standard, but without His help, we'll never be able to live it out.

At the start of Willow Creek Community Church a non-Christian attorney who helped us do some of the paperwork pulled me off to the side and said, "Bill, I have to warn you about something because I like you. You are an idealistic young guy. You are going to start this church, and you obviously think lives are going to be changed.

"I have been an attorney for twenty years, and let me tell you, people don't change. Adulterers keep committing adultery.

Greedy people get greedier. Angry people get increasingly bitter. People who are out of control stay out of control. If you hope for any fundamental change in people's lives, it is going to result in nothing but heartbreak for you."

Twenty years later, I realize that man was both right and wrong. Apart from the power of Christ, he was absolutely right. I meet with people all the time who have aspirations for turning their lives around "someday," but they are just as cranky, lustful, power hungry, and materialistic as they have always been. Without Christ in their lives, they have actually shifted toward greater degrees of unrighteousness. It's just human nature.

But I also have seen people commit their lives to Christ and then submit to a righteous God and watched as their lives became radically changed for the better. They never reached perfection, but they were at least headed in the right direction, and the end result was a radical departure from the self-serving, self-absorbed people they used to be.

The apostle Paul says, "Having been set free from sin, you became slaves of righteousness."[8] You know that tether keeping your hot-air balloon tied to the ground? It can be cut! You can watch yourself be launched into the righteousness of God by giving your life to Christ.

So then, we need to look up to God for our idea of right and wrong. We need to break our natural chains of unrighteousness by giving our lives to Christ. And finally, we need to enroll in the school of righteousness.

Enroll in the School of Righteousness

One recent morning I woke up in an ornery mood. I didn't have a reason to be ornery, I just was. I walked out the door into our garage and stumbled over my kids' shoes. I have told them a hundred times, "Put your shoes in the closet so people don't trip on them."

They forget. They are unrighteous too. In frustration, I kicked the shoes out of the way, sending our little dog scurrying for a corner. Whimpering, he gave me one of those expressions that said, "I'm going to make myself scarce because Bill looks dangerous."

As I drove to church I thought, *The dog is right. I am dangerous right now.* I had a relapse into unrighteousness. So I thought about a lesson I had learned a long time ago: When you know you are dangerous, when unrighteousness starts looking good to you, you better do something about it.

I walked into my office, got my spiral notebook, and started writing. "Dear God, I'm dangerous. My dog told me so—it was that obvious. You don't even have to be human to see it. The sad thing is, I don't even know why I'm in such a bad mood, but I know I am not going to be loving in my relationships today if something doesn't change in me. If people push me a little bit, and they will, there are going to be some problems. I don't want to be this way. I want to be a righteous man. I want to be a loving man."

I finished journaling, then took my Bible and read 1 Corinthians 13, the well-known love chapter that is often read at weddings. I was reminded that the central measuring rod by which our lives will be assessed is love. I let the Scriptures wash over me for a time, then got down on my knees and prayed. *God, I don't want to live today in unrighteousness. I don't want to wound people. I don't want to say things I will regret.*

I was even so concerned I called a friend. "I'm a little loose in the turn today," I said.

"Why?"

"I haven't figured it out yet, so stop pushing me about it!"

"Okay, okay," my friend replied.

With fresh proof that I really did have an attitude problem, my friend just talked to me. Gradually, through the spiritual disciplines and habits of yielding, writing, praying, Bible reading, and fellowship, I started to make some adjustments. I wasn't going to let an unrighteous day "just happen."

By midday, I wasn't so dangerous anymore. And by evening, I was back on course.

The point is this: We relapse so easily into unrighteousness that unless we commit ourselves to the habits and relationships that help us live rightly, we are probably going to fall back.

First Timothy 6:11 tells us to "pursue righteousness." It does not say, "Lay around until it comes your way." We have to pursue it. First Timothy 4:7 puts it another way: "Exercise yourself toward godliness."

Let me close this chapter with this one last thought. Just imagine the opportunity that is before you because you serve a righteous God. Some of you are about a third of the way through your lives. Some of you are halfway through, others of you three-quarters of the way through. Why don't you make the stretch from today to your last day a little more righteous? Why don't you do your marriage right? Why don't you do your job right? Why don't you raise your kids right?

Deep in our hearts, we want to be a righteous people, and we want to know a righteous God. We don't want a God who is capricious, who can't be counted on to do the right thing. Fortunately, the God we seek is a God who is intrinsically righteous and who will be so forever. With His example and His strength, we can share in that righteousness.

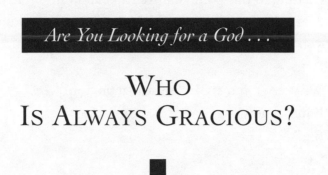

7

Are You Looking for a God...

WHO
IS ALWAYS GRACIOUS?

"Bill, I think it's going to happen. I think we're going to be able to build on our ninety acres."

Quig was (and still is) a key board member who in the early days of Willow Creek spent hundreds of hours working with the attorneys and the various municipalities around South Barrington to win the permission for us to build a church. Finally, after months of foot-dragging and question raising, it looked like the authorities were going to give us the go-ahead.

"There's just one problem," Quig warned me. "The village officials are quite nervous about creating crowded conditions and congestion in this community. It's crucial that we low-key everything while the zoning boards are passing our requirements." He caught my gaze and repeated himself, "Whatever you do, when you talk with someone, make sure you low-key it."

"No problem," I said. "I'll low-key it."

Quig held his gaze.

"Why are you looking at me?" I asked.

"I need to make this really clear. We've spent hundreds of hours getting to this point and we can't afford to blow it now." And then, to push the point even farther he said, "Tell me, what can't you say in a theater?"

"Fire."

"What can't you say in South Barrington?"

"I don't know."

"Big."

"Got it."

A few weeks later a reporter called for an interview over the phone. "You got some time to talk?" he asked.

"Sure," I said.

"Tell us about your church."

"It's a great place. A lot of people are finding Christ and finding help for their lives."

He said, "Well, like what kind of ministries do you have?"

"We have youth ministries here and we have ministries for the poor and we have ministries for singles."

He said, "It sounds like you have a lot going on."

"Well, the idea is to have a diverse inventory of ministries so that people can get all kinds of help."

"An inventory of ministries? That sounds like a retail term."

"Well, I never thought of it that way, but I guess it is. We want to have lots of places for people to get connected."

The reporter explored this concept with me for about another ten minutes and finally said, "It sounds like a religious mall."

"Well, I don't know about that, but we want to have lots of ministries and open doors for people."

"Well, thank you very much, Bill."

The next day someone walked up to me and shoved a newspaper in my face. In big, bold letters the headline read, "Religious Shopping Center Coming to South Barrington."

Quig's voice from two weeks ago came back to haunt me. *In a theater you don't say "fire" and in South Barrington you don't say "big."*

I knew Quig was going to call. I suspected that my young pastoral career had just come to an end—fired by my first church! And I would deserve it too. Quig had spent a ridiculous number of hours building rapport with the authorities, and I had ruined the whole thing with one careless interview.

Still, I had to hope. Perhaps, I thought, I might just get a severe reprimand and be given a second chance. Either way, I wasn't looking forward to the call, but I knew it was coming.

Early in the afternoon, the receptionist sent Quig's call through. The first words out of his mouth were, "You know, you could even low-key that thing back another notch if you want to."

"I'm so sorry. You have no idea how sorry I am." I didn't stop there. I went on and on until Quig stopped me and said, "Look, you're young." (He didn't say, "and stupid," but we both knew he was thinking it.) "I bet you'll never do it again. Besides, you have heart, you have vision, and"—these were the words that broke my heart—"you have a friend. I've got a bonus check and I want to take you to this Italian place for lunch. Meet me over there."

That day, I experienced the taste, feel, sight, and touch of grace. It was a radical departure from what I grew up with and a supernatural twist on the way things usually work.

Building Blisters on the Treadmill of Good Works

In this country, life as we know it is predicated on performance. As kids, we are taught that if you want something, you have to earn it. As adults, we know that if we want a sales award, we've got to go out and sell. If we want a promotion, we have to put in the long hours. If we want to succeed—be it vocationally, athletically, or financially—we've got to cover ourselves with this work ethic and make success happen for ourselves.

Based on this understanding, I spent the first half of my life attempting to please God by doing good and being good. After all, I reasoned, my diligence paid off in other areas—grades and athletics—so wouldn't my faith be the same? But soon I started wondering, *How does God grade my performance? What's the quota of good deeds, and how do I know if I'm passing or failing?*

Whenever I committed a clear-cut sin, I'd think to myself, *Oh great, all the way back to square one*, and soon I felt as if I was trying to climb an icy slope—slip once, and you slide all the way back to the bottom.

Slowly, the harrowing thought occurred to me: *I'll probably never be good enough*. I knew mercy could go only so far, and it seemed to stretch beyond my own condition. (The apostle Paul said he was the worst of sinners, but he never met me.)

In short, I was done for. At least that's what I thought, until I came face-to-face with grace. When I read in Isaiah that even my most righteous acts—my Sunday best—were like service station "grease rags," I realized that noble deeds could never get me in. Even my best fell pitifully short.

Now, this might sound odd to some of you, but the realization that it was impossible to get into heaven on my own ticket became a tremendously liberating experience for me. I realized I had to catch a different train, and that's when I was run over by a locomotive called grace. And when I first discovered the truth about grace, I opened up my hands and my heart and I prayed, *God, if You are so outrageously gracious that You would offer to save me and forgive my sin and take me to heaven on the basis of what Christ did for me on the cross . . . If You would do that for a sinner like me, and if that comes as a free gift, Lord, I receive it.*

I felt a release and a liberation unlike anything I had ever felt before. Finally, my feet weren't building blisters on the treadmill of good works. I was lifted off the tightrope of the fear of death and punishment, and instead cast upon the sure ground and security of an outrageous love that came with no strings attached. The Scripture that served as my mile-wide platform of assurance was "For by grace you have been saved through faith, and that not of yourselves; it is the gift of God, not of works, lest anyone should boast."[1]

Later, I went to a friend and asked, "Why didn't anybody tell me I could be saved by grace and not by my performance?"

She said, "Bill, we've all been trying, but you have been so determined to save yourself you couldn't hear us."

She was dead right about me. Is she right about you? Are you trying to climb a spiritual performance ladder, not realizing that the ladder will never reach to God? If so, I've got some great news for you. The God you're looking for is a gracious God.

In Psalm 103:8, we read, "The LORD is merciful and gracious, / Slow to anger, and abounding in mercy." If someone were to say, "Just show me one verse from the Bible that gives me a picture of who God is," this is the one I would point to.

Grace has changed my life, but I've come across few realities that have been so misunderstood by our culture. When people think of someone as being "gracious," they usually think nice, tolerant, sensitive, that type of thing. "Oh, what a gracious person." "What a gracious host or hostess." But what does the Bible mean when it speaks about grace? I want to spend a little time on this definition, because understanding the nature of God's grace has been the most powerful experience I've known as a Christian.

Justice, Mercy, and Grace

Bound up in who God is is an inclination to bestow benefits on undeserving people. "Nice" humans might experience an occasional desire to bestow a benefit on a very deserving person—say a boss gives a productive employee an extra day off; a hardworking student gets an extension on his paper; behaving children get to enjoy an ice cream cone on the way home from Grandma's.

But God's grace comes from an entirely different planet. No common blood flows between God's grace and human grace. God's grace is as extraordinary as human grace is ordinary. To understand this, you must first understand the relationship of justice, mercy, and grace.

Let's say you're walking down your driveway to pick up the morning paper, and you notice the fifteen-year-old kid who lives a couple of houses away. He doesn't have his driver's license yet. He has "borrowed" the family car without permission, and he's backing out of the driveway in a rushed and careless fashion. You're concerned because you know he doesn't have his license, and you're also concerned because you know there's trouble in that household.

So you watch and you listen to the tires squeal and you see the car lurch forward; the kid's head is just barely peeking out over the steering wheel. The car is all over the road, then it jerks to the right and plows through your mailbox, your bushes, and the fence that you built last summer. As the cloud of dust settles, you see the boy step out of the car with a sheepish look on his face, and you've got a decision to make. You have three choices.

Your first choice is to treat him with justice. You can give him exactly what he deserves. "All right kid, you messed up, so I'm going to call the police and they'll cite you for driving without a license. After that I'll call your parents to tell them what happened. And then you're going to have to get a job to pay for my mailbox, my bushes, and my fence."

If you treat the kid with justice, you're not a bad person. You're simply giving him exactly what he deserves—no more, no less.

However, you might choose a second option: mercy. Mercy is giving somebody a little bit less than he deserves. You say, "I'm not going to call the police, but I am going to call your parents, and we are going to establish what the mailbox costs, what the bushes cost, and what the fence costs, and you're going to pay."

If you do that, the kid ought to be very thankful because, instead of applying strict justice, you are choosing to be merciful. He's getting less punishment than he deserves.

But it's possible you might choose a third option. This option, however, doesn't square with common sense. It's risky, it could blow up in your face, and some might even call it scandalous. *You might choose to treat the kid with grace.*

"You messed up, kid. You mowed down my mailbox, you ruined my bushes, and you flattened my fence. It took me half the summer to build that fence. But I'm not going to call the police. I'm not even sure I want to get you in a whole lot of trouble with your family. As for the mailbox and the bushes and the fence, I can fix those. But how about you and me get in the car and find a place where we can sit down and have a sandwich. Then I can find out a little bit more about who you are and what's going on in your life and what the future might hold for you. Would you do that with me?"

The kid nods.

"There's just one condition," you add.

"What's that?"

"I'm driving."

What's your reaction to that last choice? You might say, "That's the stupidest thing I've ever heard in my life. All the kid is going to do is take a joyride the next day and plow someone else's mailbox down."

You know what? He might. That's the risk and scandal of grace. But it's also possible that your scandalous grace will touch that young boy at the deepest part of his soul. Your interest in his welfare and future might unlock potential he's long since forgotten, and you might witness the transformation of another life changed by grace.

All day long, we walk around assessing whether to treat people with justice, mercy, or grace. But none of them will make sense until we understand what we really deserve.

The Grace Explosion

A few years ago, a friend took me out on his boat in Southern California. As we passed through Newport Beach Harbor, I saw big, bold letters on the transom of a beautiful million-dollar yacht: *Deserved.*

Let's talk about what that guy with the million-dollar boat really deserves. (And what you and I really deserve.) Until we understand that, we'll never understand the true nature of grace.

Romans 6:23 says, "The wages of sin is death." Now here's the deal. Way back in the Garden of Eden, God said, "The day you rebel against Me, the day you shake your fist at Me and say, 'I know Your way but I'm going mine,' the day you disobey Me with that rebellious spirit, in that day you shall surely die. The wages of sin is death."

In a moral economy ruled by an absolutely holy and righteous God, when we commit cosmic treason and lie, cheat, steal, profane God's name, and violate the holiness of God, we deserve death. If we were to get straight justice from God, we'd be obliterated on the spot. God wouldn't be mean and nasty when He annihilated us—He'd be just. We couldn't shake our fist at Him and tell Him, "We don't deserve this"—because we do. It's the way He set up the world.

What if we were to receive mercy? Psalm 103:10 says, "He has not dealt with us according to our sins, / Nor punished us according to our iniquities." Because God is merciful, His policy is not "one sin, one whack." There is not a one-to-one correspondence between our sinning and dying on the spot every time, because God's amazingly merciful nature leads Him to give us less than the full punishment we deserve.

But then comes grace. Grace is an outrageous blessing bestowed freely on a totally undeserving recipient. It's scandalous. It's too good to be true. It's what makes people say, "No, that could never happen." Yet the Bible says it does happen.

Grace is a stunning and pleasant assault in which God says, "You know what I am going to do? I am going to shock people by doling out something so outrageous and irrational that when this blessing hits them it is going to cause a spiritual explosion in their heart that will change them forever."

When you know what you deserve yet you get something more wonderful than you could earn in a thousand lifetimes—*boom!*—the grace explosion happens in your heart, and you will never be the same. This is exactly what happened to the prodigal son in Luke 15. This wayward son took his father's inheritance and blew it. He did every self-destructive and God-dishonoring thing a young, rebellious man with pockets full of money could do. Some of you know exactly what that young man did.

When his debauchery, high living, and foolish choices led him so low that pigs' feed started looking good, he thought to himself, *This is justice. I'm dying in a pen full of swine, but this is what I deserve. I wasted the old man's inheritance—money that he gained through decades of hard work and right living. I violated everything I was taught and I even invented new ways to get myself into trouble. I shook my fist at God and His ways, and now I've trashed my life and I'm crawling around with pigs. If I die like this, it's not an unfair deal; I got justice.*

Yet even though he was standing in a grimy, smelly pigpen, he dared to imagine mercy—not because his sins had become any less odious, but because he had some understanding of his father's love. He couldn't get beyond mercy to grace—that hadn't even entered his mind. He just had the faith to envisage the possibility that his dad might be merciful, so he told himself, *This is what I'll do. I'll go back home. The first thing I will say to my dad is, "I am no longer worthy to be called your son." I'm only going to ask for a bunk out with the hired hands and maybe some food, and I'll work for it.*

Never in his wildest dreams did he imagine what was waiting for him. This delinquent son got a huge love blessing that was completely out of line: the embrace of his father, a ring on his finger, a celebration with his friends and family, the feast of his life. It was irrational.

Boom! That kid was forever changed by a stunning assault of grace. I doubt he went out two months later with money in his pockets to the same town to do the same stuff to wind up in the same pen. The kid who would have done that was dead. He had been blown apart by grace.

Until this explosion occurs in your heart you'll never really understand grace. You have no idea of its power or its cost. Remember, God didn't just wink at sin. Jesus, His Son, paid the price to satisfy His justice requirements. Because of that transaction, God can offer the gift of forgiveness and salvation and say, "Here it is, grace to you who want it, who need it, who will claim it."

Do you see grace more clearly now? It is undeserved. It comes from the heart of a gracious God who wants to stun you and overwhelm you with a gift you don't deserve—salvation, adoption, a spiritual ability to use in kingdom service, answered prayer, the church, His presence, His wisdom, His guidance, His love. The truth is, we don't deserve a single one of these, much less a million-dollar yacht, but God is so unbelievably gracious that He gives us eternal blessings so rich, they make yachts look like trinkets placed in Happy Meals.

■

The Blessings of Grace

The pardon that God offers is an equal opportunity offer. God makes this offer to spectacular sinners, boring sinners, nasty sinners, proper sinners, secret sinners, educated sinners, uneducated sinners, religious sinners, and atheistic sinners. The truth is, God delights in offering His pardon.

When this grace comes your way, the first thing you feel is enormous relief. "Ah, forgiveness is available. I won't have to pay the rest of my life for this mistake." My relief was closer to euphoria. I had tried so hard that the thought of an unearned pardon was overwhelmingly good news.

The next thing you feel is the possibility of reconciliation. When the infamous "religious mall" headline came out, my fear wasn't limited to losing my job. I had grown to treasure my relationship with Quig, and I thought, *It's all over now. He'll never want to speak to me again.* But what happened? Quig invited me to lunch.

I felt hope. Grace-giving does that. It relieves people from having to pay and pay and pay. There was nothing I could do to take back my comments to the reporter; there was no way I could "repay" Quig for the hundreds of hours of his time that I had placed in serious jeopardy. But grace covers all that, and more. It invites people back into a relationship with God and others they've offended. In a system in which there's grace, dreams—not nightmares—define our lives.

This, however, is what I call the "scandal of grace," the very sticking point that keeps people from embracing it.

The Scandal of Grace

I once had lunch with a business executive with whom I'd been building a relationship. I asked for his napkin and his pen. The pen looked as if it cost at least two hundred dollars, so I knew I'd have his undivided attention if I used his pen instead of mine. He wasn't about to let it out of his sight!

Taking his pen, I wrote *God* at the top of the napkin, then drew a line pointing down. Pointing to the word *God*, I said, "Here's God's standard of holiness. Here's a line," and following the line downward, "and down here are the bad people of the world. Put an *x* somewhere on this line where you belong on the morality ladder."

He did, and then I continued. "The gap between your *x* and the holiness of God is precisely the problem. You have fallen short of the standards of God's holiness by your own admission. That gap is what you will stand accountable for on the day of judgment."

I turned the napkin over and said, "All people tend to do one of two things with that shortfall." I drew a line across the middle, then wrote, "The Moral Self-Improvement Plan."

"This is when people spend the rest of their life trying to bring their *x* mark up a little bit higher. The Bible says it doesn't work even if you give yourself a hundred lifetimes. You can't get up to the place of moral perfection if you're a fallen human being."

Then on the other side of that dividing line, I wrote, "The Grace Plan."

The guy said, "What's that?"

"You're not going to believe it. In the 'Grace Plan' God says, 'I see the gap and I know you can't make it by your own human strength, so I'm going to send Christ, My Son, to pay for the shortfall. Salvation and adoption into My family will be made available to you as a gift.'"

"Which of the two are you in?" I asked. "The Grace Plan or the Moral Self-Improvement Plan?"

"I'm in the Moral Self-Improvement Plan."

I agreed. "From all I see of you, I think you are too."

I will never forget what happened next. He looked up and searched my eyes. In that one, five-second glance, he was thinking, *If only what you are saying is true. If I felt that today I could just abandon the self-improvement plan and receive grace as a free gift for an undeserving sinner like me, it would change everything.*

This "sanctified suspicion" is what keeps so many people away from Christianity. If somebody tells us all we have to do is show up and get a free car, we know it can't be true, so how can we expect a free ticket to heaven? This grace business just sounds too good, too easy. Successful people who have worked long and hard to obtain their place in society and their nice house and their big office and their imported cars simply don't want to believe that God would *give* them a place in heaven. "Nothing gets handed to you on a silver platter," they insist, and most of the time, they are right. But in this case, they are tragically wrong.

That's why when you open your life up to Christ and you experience the grace explosion, you will be pelted with the shrapnel of relief. In the back of your mind, you *knew* you couldn't earn your way into heaven, and now you realize you don't have to. Instead of defining your relationship with God by your own efforts, you'll watch in amazement as God draws near of His own accord. Hope will nourish your soul: *Maybe with God's help I can start my life over again. Maybe I can walk with a clean slate into a different kind of future.*

Actually, there's no "maybe" about it. It just comes down to grace, and it's true. It's also enduring.

Sustained by Grace

It's one thing to sneak inside the ballpark; it's another thing to stay there. Some of you might be thinking, *Okay, so grace can*

make me a Christian, but how do I stay one? That's the catch, isn't it? It's one thing to say a prayer, accept God's free and gracious gift, and then maintain our state of obedience—for about one hour. But what about next week, when my spouse and kids forget to pick up after themselves, when my boss blames me for a coworker's mistake, when my neighbor's dog barks half the night—how can I be gracious *then*?

First, you have to remember the initial cost of God's investment in you—nothing less than the life of His only Son. God didn't just "bet the farm" on your salvation. He wagered His own flesh and blood.

Once God has given us His Son, do you think He will scrimp on the extras?

We're not only saved by grace, but the Bible says we're *sustained* by grace. God's promise of eternal life includes a rider that offers a certain quality of life. Jesus says, "I have come that they may have life, and that they may have it more abundantly."[2] The psalmist cries out, "What shall I render to the LORD / For all His benefits toward me?"[3]

I used to try to explain this concept to my son by saying, "Todd, it's like this. God decides to buy us a Buick. There's no reason for this purchase, He just wants to give us a gift. Do you think such a gracious God is then going to hold back on the options? I don't think so! He's going to say, 'Make sure it has a good stereo. Sunroof? Sure. Leather seats? Why not? I want to embarrass this guy!'"

I don't know if this illustration ever really sunk into Todd's heart, but he'd often request to hear the story about the Buick and the cool stereo!

That's exactly what Paul is saying in Romans 8:32: "He who did not spare His own Son, but delivered Him up for us all, how shall He not with Him also freely give us all things?"

Have no fear about entering by grace and then treading water by human effort. Once God lets us in, He keeps us in. He won't hold anything back. We'll have everything we need to live a life of obedience and commitment.

■

Senseless Acts of Graciousness

Let me give you one last thought. We've talked a lot about the transforming nature of *receiving* grace, but now I want to say a word about the revolutionary aspect of *giving* grace. We're pretty good at spreading justice: "You bump me and I bump you back." Occasionally, when we're in a good mood, we might flirt with being merciful: "You bump me, and I'll bump you back a little less forcefully." But Jesus would like us to unleash outrageous acts of random graciousness.

In Matthew 20 Jesus told a parable of a landowner who hired guys in the early morning to work a full day in the vineyard. And then he went back and hired guys late in the morning, then early in the afternoon, and even late in the afternoon. Finally he hired another crew of guys with one hour left in the day.

When the working day ended, he paid all of them the same amount. And the people who had worked an entire day said, "Wait. You gave us a bum deal!"

And the landowner replied, "Did I? When you asked me if you could work for me, I promised you a full day's wage for a full day's work. That's justice. I've kept my word."

■

They had to reconsider. His logic was impeccable. "Okay, I guess we're square," they admitted. "But what about the guys who just worked the one hour?"

The landowner said, "I just wanted to perform a random, senseless act of grace. I just wanted to give them something that would make them run home to their spouses and cry out, 'Do you believe what has come my way? I worked one hour and got paid for an entire day. It's outrageous. Let's party!'"

If we treat each other with justice, we're just being square with each other. We're not going to touch one another's heart or soul very deeply. If we're occasionally merciful with each other, we'll warm up the relational temperature a bit. But it won't be all that transforming.

However, every once in a while, if we perform a random, senseless act of grace-giving we can enter a new dimension of living. If we forgive somebody of something when we could easily hold it against them; if we take an IOU that someone owes us and write a note that says, "Paid in full" (which are the same words that Jesus wrote on the sin list of your life); if we tell that person, "I want to set you free as I've been set free," we'll discover the power and reality of grace.

Here's a challenge: Every once in a while, give some of your time away—as a young single mom from my church told me recently. She said, "I only have a couple of weeks of vacation, and you know what I'm going to do? It's the craziest thing. I'm going to spend one week building a home for another single mom in the Dominican Republic with our International Ministries."

"Why would you do that?"

"If you knew how God had changed my life, you'd understand."

Give some of your talent or money away. Embarrass someone with an extravagant gift.

In church we sing, "Amazing grace, how sweet the sound that saved a wretch like me," but do we really know what we're singing about? Are we open to this type of grace, a grace that is scandalous in its offer and explosive in its power to change human lives?

Will you open your heart and take grace in for its richness, its fullness, and its pardon? Will you? Will you allow its work to purge your heart and to cleanse your soul and make you more loving? Will you commit yourself to doing random, senseless acts of graciousness every now and then that will send someone running back home shouting, "You won't believe it!"?

I hope you will. Because God's grace is real, and you will be blown away by the difference that grace can make.

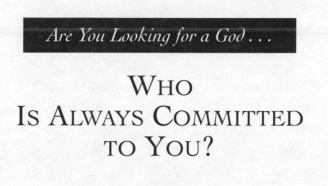

8

Are You Looking for a God...

WHO IS ALWAYS COMMITTED TO YOU?

It was late at night—ten or eleven o'clock—and I was bone weary. Although I was only a junior in high school, I had been driving a fully loaded semitrailer rig for sixteen hours. I was in the middle of nowhere, but that was okay. The name of the town didn't matter, even the state didn't matter—they were just destination points on the route map. The only thing that mattered to me was the bright red sign announcing "Truck Stop." I pulled into the parking lot, shut down the rig, and made my way into the diner, choosing a seat in the drivers' section.

I saw him sitting in a corner booth, a cigarette dangling between two fingers, wispy curls of steam rising from his extra-black coffee. He took off his baseball cap to run his fingers through his hair. I mistakenly thought he was waving at me, so I said "Hi," and he said "Hi" back, and then he started telling me the story I had come to know so well. Their names were always different, and the states they crossed and seasons they conquered changed, but the gist of the stories of veteran drivers was as predictable as a paperback romance novel.

"Got two million miles on that baby out there in the lot," he said, pointing toward the window. Outside I saw the commanding presence of a White Freightliner. It was difficult to tell under the lights, but the truck looked as if it was at least fifteen years old.

"Still starts without a boost in twenty-below weather," the veteran droned on. He took a sip of coffee, licked his lips, and added, "Had eighty thousand pounds on her when I took her through the Smoky Mountains, the only truck that made it. Yep. And she was the only truck on I-80 during the blizzard of 1958 . . ."

He smiled at me. "You were probably in diapers then," he guessed.

Not quite, but I figured that a man who has driven enough miles to circumnavigate the globe several times had earned the privilege of underestimating my age. And I enjoyed my conversation with him.

I didn't stay with my father's produce company that long, but I drove enough miles and drank sufficient cups of coffee in enough truck stops to become familiar with the veteran drivers who regaled us rookies with amazing stories of mechanical reliability.

When talking with such a driver, it was virtually impossible to silence his praise for his truck. However much you might try to argue the merits of the newest rigs, or however intricate your knowledge of the latest advancements and improvements in truck engineering, you could never sever the bonds that had been formed in the visceral levels of a man's soul when he has been dependent on a truck to get him through the worst weather and over the highest mountain range.

The trucks had proven themselves faithful in the snow, in the desert heat, and under heavy loads, and the bond between man and machine that was forged through such events outlasted just about any other commitment the drivers experienced. The country might turn communist, the wife might find some other man, the kids might become delinquent—but these veteran drivers could *always* count on their truck.

We live in a world in which such faithfulness is almost an anomaly. In another twenty years, it might even be relegated to museums. You know what I'm referring to: Spouses trade in their marriages, employers trade employees, athletes leave one team as soon as another team promises a few more dollars, pastors, on average, leave their church every four years. . . . It's startling how unfaithful our society has become.

Things have gotten so bad that sociologists and writers are now referring to this generation as "the generation that wants to keep its options open, the nonjoiners, the commitment-free generation."

And yet, commitment, traditionally, is the very stuff that makes us strong, that helps us hold everything else together.

Against this backdrop—a humanity created to depend on commitment yet running from it as if it were the most deadly plague imaginable—I want to draw your attention to a God who knows faithfulness and who knows commitment like no one else.

■

God Is a Commitment-Maker and a Commitment-Keeper

When Todd was five years old, he asked me to move my car so he could get his bike out of the garage.

"Dad, move your car!" he said.

"I will, Todd, I will," I kept saying.

Five minutes later, Todd came back to me and said, "Dad, you really better move your car or you're going to be in trouble with a capital *P*."

"Don't you mean *T*, Todd?"

"Whatever."

Todd knew I had made a commitment to move that car—"I will, Todd, I will"—but he had understandable concerns about whether I would keep my commitment.

We need have no such concerns about God. He is eager to make commitments, and He delights in being faithful to them.

All the way back in Genesis, God makes a startling promise to a childless man named Abram. "I will make you a great nation; / I will bless you / And make your name great; / And you shall be a blessing . . . / And in you all the families of the earth shall be blessed."[1]

Abram lived happily with the hope of this promise for several years, but as the seasons passed and a few more wrinkles showed up on his forehead and a few more aches crept into his bones, Abram began having second thoughts. The next time God appeared to Abram, he took the opportunity to remind God that His earlier promise hadn't yet been fulfilled. "Look, You have given me no offspring . . . !"[2]

Instead of trying to verbally convince Abram of His faithfulness, God did something that is absolutely stunning when you understand the nature of commitment-making in Abram's days. To renew His commitment to Abram, God asked Abram to split a young heifer, a goat, a ram, a turtledove, and a pigeon and lay the sides out, with a pathway in between the split carcasses.

It might sound gory, but Abram knew exactly what God was doing. When two people made an agreement in the days before lawyers and triplicate copies, they sometimes would walk in between the two sides of animal carcasses, giving each other a clear picture of what would happen should the commitment be broken. "Look left, and look right. If you break this commitment, you'll be split down the middle just like one of these animals."

The difference on this occasion, however, was that God sent Abram into a deep sleep and then, symbolized by a burning torch, God alone passed through those carcasses. In essence, God was telling Abram, "I promise to do this. I'll make the commitment official. It's going to happen. You can count on it."

God's commitment with Abram (whom He later named Abraham) was just one of many commitments He has made. God promised Noah that there would never be another worldwide flood. God once made a commitment to David, saying, "I'm going to lift the nation of Israel to world significance." He kept that promise and Israel became a world-dominating power. God also made a commitment to Solomon, David's son, promising him he would get to play a role that even his father could not play: Solomon would build the temple of God and usher in the most prosperous period of Israel's life before the coming of the Messiah. God kept His promise, and Solomon built the temple.

God also made a commitment to Mary and Joseph, the parents of Jesus: They would have a "supernatural" Child. And every time that Child did something a little unusual, like skip out on the family vacation to play "Jeopardy" with the Jewish rabbis, they were reminded that this, indeed, was no ordinary Child.

God the Father made many commitments to Jesus, the most important being the assurance that His redemptive work on the cross would satisfy the requirements of justice and make salvation available to any undeserving person who asks for it.

Just ponder the implications for a moment. Jesus risked everything, and I mean *everything*—exchanging the glories and pleasures of heaven for thirty-three years of life on this planet and death by crucifixion—to accomplish one aim: our salvation. He risked all of this *based on the promise of His Father* that His actions and sacrifice would be fruitful. Jesus knew His Father was faithful, so He willingly risked all.

God promised the early church in Jerusalem that they would be the launching pad for churches that would someday spread all around the world. At first, such a thought was almost laughable—as laughable as a childless man becoming the father of many nations. But God kept His word, and today, that little church in Jerusalem has produced little communities of faith in almost every city, town, and village around the world.

God spoke all of these commitments ahead of time. He was willing to go "on record" because it is in God's nature to be faithful. You can count on the fulfillment of His promises as surely as you can count on the sun rising and setting each day.

God's faithfulness to His commitments means everything to me. I am able to relax about my future because God has gone on record to assure me He will walk with me through the dark, uncertain forests of tomorrow.[3] When I consider my existence beyond the grave, I am filled with confidence and gratitude because God has made an inviolable commitment to take me to heaven on the merits of Christ.[4] And I know beyond all doubt that grace is available to me when I fail.[5]

Tens of millions of people buy United States savings bonds, not because they pay more than other investments—their interest is relatively poor—but because they are backed by the

United States government and therefore relatively secure. Well, I "buy" Scripture's promises because they are backed by nothing less than the inherent character and nature of God, and absolutely nothing is more secure than that.

When I look deep inside the center of my life these days, I find that there is a serenity of soul. This serenity didn't come from meditating. It didn't result from years of laboriously accumulating good works. It doesn't emanate from self-awareness or esoteric wisdom. It has been birthed by the commitment-making, commitment-keeping nature of God.

I thought about this "serenity" when I was out on a sailing trip with three other men from our church. After we sailed past the sight of land and past the sight of any other boats, when we reached an expanse of ocean that was completely our own, we started playing worship music tapes at *full volume*. The chorus of one of our favorite tapes boomed off the waves, "He will not let you fall, He will not let you fall, He is never weary and He will not let you fall."

None of us were singers, but we belted out the words as loudly as if we were rock-and-roll singers at a modern-day Woodstock. "He will not let you fall, He will not let you fall, He is never weary and He will not let you fall."

For the rest of the weekend, whenever someone was grinding a winch or trimming a sail, someone would yell out, "Hey, will He let you fall?"

"No!" he'd shout back. "He won't let me fall!" You either!

When we spoke this way, we weren't competing with Pollyanna for naive optimism, nor were we trying to cultivate some type of feel-good but meaningless assurance. Our certainty was based on the rock-solid character of God and it sent peace into the deepest recesses of our souls.

Such peace comes only from experience, actually witnessing the commitment-keeping character of God. Whenever a church is singing the hymn "Great Is Thy Faithfulness," I like to look around and see the gray-haired people singing with such conviction that their veins are bulging. Their faces are filled with a confident smile, and each syllable is punctuated with absolute belief. Middle-aged people frequently sing the same song with an interested, perhaps hopeful belief. Adolescents and children tend to sing it with distraction and borderline boredom.

Why? The older people have experienced God's faithfulness and promise-keeping to them, and they are certain that what they are singing is true. Like the trucker bearing witness to his rig, these people are proclaiming God's commitment and nobody could persuade them otherwise. To them, God's faithfulness isn't a theory or a theological technicality. It's the story of their lives: "Great is Thy faithfulness, Lord unto me." And the older I get I find myself singing this hymn with increasing gusto.

This faithfulness of God leads us to our second point. Because we have been made in the image of God, God fully expects that His people will also become commitment-makers and commitment-keepers.

■

God Expects Us to Make and Keep Commitments

On a sunny August morning, three different couples prepare for a weekend of "sailing." One couple get out of their car, the one with the license plate holder that reads, "I'd Rather Be Sailing," and begin to haul their provisions to the boat. It takes them several trips to carry their picnic basket and the rest of their gear to their craft. Once aboard, they change their clothes, turn on the music, and then spend the better part of the day lounging around on the boat (which is still tied to the dock), reading and napping and talking. They sleep in the cabin Saturday night, and on Sunday morning go through roughly the same routine of the previous day, cleaning up the sailboat, reading and napping. Then about four o'clock, they pack everything up and drive back home.

The second couple get to their boat early on Saturday morning. They travel to the same marina, they have the same license plate frame, they bring the same gear, turn on the same music, socialize a bit, but then do something somewhat odd: They start up the motor. They untie the ropes. They back out of their slip and cruise around the harbor.

The couple may spend an hour looking at the other boats in the harbor and then drop anchor to cook a dinner meal. That evening, they may even venture out by the breakwater, to gaze out on the open seas, but then come back in, sleep on the sailboat, and repeat the whole process on Sunday.

The third couple get to their boat early on Saturday, bring their gear aboard, back out of the slip, and head straight for the breakwater. As they're heading out, they hoist the sails, and when the wind fills them, they shut off the motor and enter the open sea. They hear the sails straining and the water rushing along the hull. They feel the swells rising up underneath them, and they keep going until the sight of land is lost. They spend the entire night out on the seas, cooking in spite of the motion of the boat underneath them. They use a flashlight at night to look at the charts and to keep their bearings. And then they come back into the harbor late Sunday night.

On Monday morning, each couple will be asked, "What did you do this weekend?" and each couple will give the same answer, "We went sailing." But did they really do the same thing?

It's like that with our commitments, isn't it? Take, for instance, the commitment between a man and a woman. Some couples will promise to be committed to each other for a night of romance, but they make no pretense that they will leave the dock of autonomy or independence. In fact, they're not even going to untie the boat.

Another couple might make a deeper commitment. Maybe they'll agree to stay faithful to each other "as long as their love shall last." Perhaps they'll even move in together and share the bills. In this, they're willing to motor around the harbor of relationship for a little while, but they never go so far as to lose sight of the land or to seriously venture into the high seas of commitment.

Yet a third couple might enter into a permanent commitment called marriage. They leave the dock of autonomy far behind and even pass through the harbor of casual relationship, reaching the high seas of commitment. No matter how rough the weather, they rule out the option of returning to the dock. They came prepared to sail, and sail they will.

The same analogy is true of faith. Some people "play" at being a Christian. They show up at church a couple of times a month, drop a five-dollar bill into the offering, and do their best to look religious, but they never untie their boat. They always manage to maintain a connection with the safety of the shoreline. Others attend church every week, boost their offerings, and occasionally even show up to volunteer for something. They're willing to motor around the harbor and "experiment" with dependence on God, but since they stop short of the open water, they never really know what it would be like to trust God deeply and fully.

The really committed leave the safety of the harbor, accept the risk of the open seas of faith, and set their compasses for the place of total devotion to God and whatever life adventures He plans for them. These are the people who eventually experience the commitment-making and -keeping nature of God. These are the ones who will someday sing "Great is Thy faithfulness" at the top of their lungs.

During Jesus' teaching ministry, His pattern was to throw open the gates of the kingdom and say, "Anyone who will repent and profess faith in God can come." He openly invited people into His family, committed Himself to forgiving their sins, and offered His ongoing protection. But then, invariably— once they became members of the family—He would set about to restructure the basic commitments of their lives. "Now, let's get serious," He would say.

Let's look at some of the commitments that Jesus calls us to, particularly how they are sometimes evidenced in the life of a remarkable man named Paul.

Committed to God

Jesus said, "Seek first the kingdom of God and His righteousness, and all these things shall be added to you."[6] Jesus is saying, "When you discover the glorious news that I am committed to you, spend a while basking in that truth, but then make a commitment back to Me. In fact, I want this to be the primary commitment in your life, the first and foremost commitment you make above every other. I will be your God, but you must be intentional about being My daughter or son."

Nowhere was this commitment more evident than it was in the life of the apostle Paul. After Paul's conversion on the Damascus road, God called Paul to a life of total devotion to Him. Before meeting Jesus, by all accounts Paul appeared to be headed for a stellar career. He willingly gave it all up, however, and embarked on a faith adventure that would not only change the course of the rest of his life, but the entire course of human history.

Committed to Making a Difference

Jesus said, "You are the salt of the earth. Don't lose the saltiness. If you lose it, how is it good for anything but to be thrown out and trampled?"[7] Here Jesus is saying, "You once lived without a commitment to making a difference with your life, but now you must agree to become My change agent in the world."

Paul's zeal to change the world was so great that his enemies accused him and the other disciples of turning "the world upside down."[8] In an age in which both sea and land travel came at a frightening cost—highway robbers on land, shipwrecks at sea—Paul's travels were stunning. He logged over two thousand miles on land and at least that much by sea. He founded a number of churches, wrote voluminous letters (and thus a significant portion of the New Testament), and endured countless indignities in his quest to bring faith in Christ to unbelieving and frequently hostile crowds. His missionary zeal to change people's lives has been unequaled in the history of the church.

Paul left the world a radically different place. Before his conversion, the Christian faith was confined to just a few cities around Jerusalem. By the time he died, the civilized world was saturated with little pockets of faith—most of them planted by Paul.

God calls us to be committed to Him, to be committed to making a difference, and to be committed to reconciliation.

Committed to Reconciliation

In Matthew 5:23–24, Jesus talks about the formation of a new commitment in the lives of His followers. In effect, Jesus is saying, "Some of you used to be pretty casual about your relationships. If one started to break down, you discarded it like yesterday's newspaper. Now, all of that must change. I want you to be committed to becoming reconciled with every person in your life, as much as it is within your power to do so."

The apostle Paul answered Jesus' challenge. He often put his life in jeopardy by insisting on the destruction of the religious, social, and cultural walls that separated the Jews from the Gentiles. Among the many accusations leveled at Paul, the Jews frequently added that he "brought Greeks into the temple and has defiled this holy place."[9] Paul did this because he adopted Jesus' passion for reconciliation. He sought to break down every form of prejudice, eventually penning one of the most eloquent and moving passages in all of Scripture: "There is neither Jew nor Greek, there is neither slave nor free, there is neither male nor female; for you are all one in Christ Jesus."[10]

When Christ calls Paul—and us—to become reconcilers, He is not only stretching our faith, but He is being merciful toward us. None of us want to look in the rearview mirror at the end of our lives and see a huge relational graveyard that we caused by a stubborn spirit and our unwillingness to swallow our pride enough to reconcile broken relationships.

■

God Grieves over Our Broken Commitments

As a pastor, I am well aware of how many people have been severely wounded and spiritually crippled through the breaking of a commitment. I met a woman at a banquet once who told me that after twenty-five years of marriage, her husband said, "I have two things to tell you: I've had multiple affairs throughout the course of our marriage, and I am currently in love with another woman."

Still reeling from the betrayal, the woman braced herself as her husband added, "And second, along the way, I've made some bad investments that you knew nothing about. We are now officially bankrupt." With that, he announced he was moving out and she was on her own.

There was a long moment of silence before I asked, "How did you handle that?"

"Not very well," she said quietly. With tears in her eyes she managed to whisper, "I don't think I will ever recuperate."

From conversations such as this one I have become intimately familiar with the human pain suffered as a result of broken commitments, but what has surprised me even more is my growing understanding of God's broken heart over our broken commitments to Him. Do you want to break God's heart? Here's a simple recipe: Simply break your word.

Hosea's Story

The Old Testament book of Hosea is a chronicle of the pain that unfaithfulness causes God. "I have a charge to bring against you," the Lord says through Hosea. "There is no faithfulness in this land." God was saying here, "When I made a commitment to form you into a nation and adopt you as My family, we made many promises to each other. The only problem is, I'm the only One keeping My word. You are banking your life on Me keeping My commitments, and I will. But you must keep yours as well."

To dramatize how wounded God feels at this betrayal, He instructs Hosea to do one of the strangest things ever asked by God in all of Scripture. God tells Hosea to visit the red-light district, pick out a prostitute, and marry her.

Theological niceties aside, can you imagine Hosea's reaction? Hosea is a God-honoring, pure-hearted man, yet God asks him to share his bed with a woman who has been used and abused to such an extent that she is a living portrait of unfaithfulness. How many vows were broken in her bed? How many families were torn apart in her arms?

Yet Hosea obediently finds a prostitute named Gomer and offers to give her the honor, dignity, and respect of becoming his wife. Gomer is shocked but delighted and eagerly follows her husband to her new home and an entirely new life. For the first time, the sexual act isn't a way to make money, it becomes a way to express affection and create a family. And as the years pass, Hosea gives Gomer even more than his house, his money, and his children. He gives her his heart.

The marriage, strange as it was, really seems to be working, until one day when Hosea comes home to an empty house. The children are by themselves and Gomer is nowhere to be found. A sick feeling spreads through Hosea's gut. Somehow, he just knows where she is, but he doesn't want to believe it. Rushing out the door, he heads toward the red-light district and then stops short when he reaches the outskirts. He sees Gomer on the street corner, her arms around another man, leading him into a house of prostitution.

Hosea is devastated. "What could that man give her that I couldn't?" he cries out. "If she wanted money, why didn't she ask me for it? If she wanted love, were my arms not as warm and tender as his?"

Somehow, Hosea makes it back to his house and fights off the temptation to burn the whole place down in his rage. But the story doesn't end here. God speaks to him and says, "I want you to go back to the red-light district, find Gomer's pimp, buy her back, and bring her home."

"Yeah, right, God, good one. What do You *really* want me to do?"

"I want you to go get Gomer. Do as I say."

Hosea is shocked that God would even *consider* asking him to do such a thing. "She already slam-dunked my heart once!" he protests. "If I take her home and we get involved again . . ." He stops. "To be honest, God, if she breaks my heart a second time, it'll be broken for good."

You know how God responds? "Now you know how I feel! I have kept all My promises. I told My people, 'I will be your God. I will love you, care for you, nurture you, always be there for you, and make you strong. I will even forgive your sin and take you to heaven some day.' But look how they've treated Me!

"Hosea, you have a broken heart because someone you loved broke her commitment to you. She violated your trust. I have taken thousands of those hits. My heart is riddled with the bullets of betrayal and unfaithfulness."

We've All Been Gomers

The book of Hosea moves elements in my soul unlike any other passage in Scripture. Why? I know I have been a Gomer to God. I have sat in church and pledged, *God, I am going to leave that sin* or *God, I am going to take action on this; I promise I will.* Time passes, and months later I realize that I haven't stopped doing what I said I'd stop doing and I haven't started doing what I said I would commit myself to.

God doesn't respond to my unfaithfulness with the callous enjoyment of a police officer who scribbles out a speeding ticket to meet his quota for the day. He doesn't view my disobedience with the curious detachment of an anthropologist. That's not it at all. When I read Hosea, I realize that my disobedience knocks the emotional wind out of God. He grieves deeply over my unfaithfulness, as a husband grieves over an adulterous wife.

Because so much is at stake, the vows and covenants we make to God should be made thoughtfully and followed through heroically. The vows we make in front of a church to our spouse are really vows made *to God*, and God takes them personally. The vows we make in a small group when we covenant to meet together and help keep each other fired-up spiritually are vows registered in the very heart of God. Sure, there is forgiveness for broken vows, but once we realize that our unfaithfulness breaks the heart of God, we'll be loathe to inflict such anguish on One who has shown us such kindness.

The good news behind all this is that just as our unfaithfulness brings great grief to our God, so our faithfulness can send joy cascading into His heart.

■

God Delights in Commitment-Keeping

Trivia question: Where is the Baseball Hall of Fame? *Cooperstown, New York.* How about the Basketball Hall of Fame? *Springfield, Maryland.* How about the Football Hall of Fame? *Canton, Ohio.* How about the Bowling Hall of Fame? *St. Louis.* (What else are you going to do in St. Louis?) How about the Daredevil Hall of Fame? Very appropriately, it's located in

■

Niagara Falls (there are only about three guys in it, but it's there).

Where is the Commitment-Making and Commitment-Keeping Hall of Fame located in the Bible? *Hebrews 11.* This Hall of Fame contains the well-known all-stars such as Noah and Abraham and Moses, but also people like Enoch and Barak and Jephthah and Rahab. These commitment-makers "subdued kingdoms, . . . obtained promises, . . . quenched the violence of fire, escaped the edge of the sword" and proved themselves "valiant in battle" (vv. 33–34). It's not that they didn't have their share of challenges. In fact, they were tortured, scourged, stoned, sawn in two, tempted and they even "wandered about . . . destitute, afflicted, tormented" (vv. 35–37).

But they each kept their promises to God, and that's how they made it into the Commitment-Keeping Hall of Fame. Rahab promised the Israelite spies that she would hide them, and she did. Barak promised to fight the king of Canaan, even though his army was greatly outnumbered, and he made good on his commitment, pursuing the defeated army until not a single soldier was left.

These heroes made solid, honorable, thoughtful commitments to God. Many of them gave up their lives before they gave in on their commitments, and God was so delighted and enthralled with their faithfulness that He made sure their names would be recorded forever.

These heroes were ordinary folks—not superstars. Rahab, in fact, had a very checkered past. Barak, before going into battle, was actually a little frightened and insisted that Deborah accompany him. Even though he commanded thousands of men, he was reluctant to enter conflict without the strong woman of God accompanying him. But both Rahab and Barak overcame their personal weaknesses. They said, "God, I'll do it," and then kept their word.

This heavenly hall of fame is still inducting members— maybe even you and me. We may never achieve great wealth or fame in the eyes of the world. Our obituaries on earth may never be larger than a classified ad. But our commitment to God can place our names on a hall of fame that will still be shining thousands of years after people have forgotten football records, stardom, or worldly success.

How can we do this? We can begin by writing down a half-dozen fundamental commitments that we want to orient our life around. This chapter mentions several that Jesus specifically addressed, but if we read carefully through the New Testament, we can find even more. We then need to review the list regularly to remind ourselves, "This is *who* I am committed to. This is *what* I am committed to. This is *how* I want to orient my life."

Next, we can take advantage of the commitment helpers that God has given to us: the Holy Spirit, the Bible, spiritual disciplines, and accountability groups. All of us need people who will spur us on by saying, "You kept that commitment! I'm proud of you!" We also need people in our lives who, when we've broken a commitment, remind us that with God's help we can do better . . . and should. That kind of accountability often inspires us to stay true to our word the next time.

But the best way to make it into the Hall of Fame of Commitment is to become more and more acquainted with our commitment-making and commitment-keeping God. The more we understand who He is and the more we chase out our ignorance of His nature, the more closely we'll be conformed to His image. Scripture reminds us that we will become more like God "when we see Him as He is."

I want to take you back to the truck stop in the middle of nowhere. Churches can be like truck stops when you think about it—people on a journey, gathering together to get "fed" and "rested" and "refueled." And hopefully many years from now you will be able to say, "I've traveled three decades with God, and He's never let me down. Got me through a job transition. Got me through a tough stretch in my marriage and a bad scare with my daughter's health . . . He's never let me down."

When you reach that level of belief in the faithfulness of God, don't be surprised if you start talking to anyone who stops long enough to have a cup of coffee at an adjoining table in a restaurant. When you get to that point, you'll have found the delight of your soul, because in a world where faithlessness and broken promises are pandemic, the God we are looking for is a God who makes and keeps commitments.

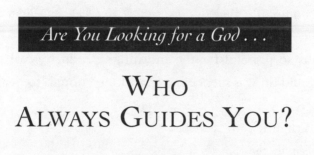

9

Are You Looking for a God . . .

WHO ALWAYS GUIDES YOU?

I was on a roll! I had spent the morning at a little restaurant down by the marina where I often go to study. God's voice had been so fresh, so vibrant, and I felt so alive it was incredible. Some days, a sermon comes out of you like a sliver deeply imbedded in a finger—eventually you get it out, but you bleed and you hurt and you wince until the pesky little thing is delivered.

But other times—and today was one of those times—sermons come in like waves. You're a surfer riding them to shore, and in such moments, preparing sermons is such a joy you can't imagine being anything but a pastor.

With the exuberant rush of a good morning's work behind me, I put on my running clothes and left our cottage for my usual six-mile run. I quickly settled into my normal gait when I spotted a familiar elderly man up ahead. I don't know how many times I had passed by him as he pulled cans out of the garbage behind the yacht club.

I kept running, another mile behind me now, and as the stiffness worked its way out of my legs, I began praying, *Lord, I invite You to speak to me this moment. If You have something to say, I want to hear it.*

I was so grateful for the morning's productivity, I felt the least I could do was silence my heart long enough to hear God's voice.

And then it came.

Remember the garbage picker?

Yeah. How could I forget? I see him practically every day.

If you see him again, love him.

God's words were gentle, but I felt as if I was having a spiritual heart attack. By urging me to love that man, God was also kindly rebuking me for *not* loving him in the past. Instantly, my thoughts were penetrated by the parable of the good Samaritan, and God's voice just about finished me off.

Hybels, you're just like the priest, except that you didn't walk around the wounded man, you ran *around him. You're off in your little corner of the world, preparing a message for thousands of people, yet you run around the one person I want you to express kindness to right now.*

I was so overcome by shame, I almost stopped running. I thought, *I don't like this listening to God anymore.* A few steps later, I said to myself, "Maybe I should go back to just talking to God. It's a lot safer!"

Listening to God is risky business. When Moses was an old man, God called out, "Hey, Moses, I want you to come up to Me on the mountain."

"How come?" Moses asked.

"I want you to die up here."

Pause. Silence.

"Hey, God, how about we meet in the valley?"

Ever feel that way? I have. In fact, I think most everyone who has listened to God faithfully has heard some pretty tough stuff. By tugging at my conscience, God won't let me get cold or distant with my wife, calloused with my kids, or cocky with my staff.

And yet, I have come to treasure these times of correction, the moments when God's voice comes into my life like a tidal wave, not only rearranging the furniture but entirely displacing my comfortable house.

Why? By now you know my most treasured friend is God. And the Bible says, "Faithful are the wounds of a friend."[1] God's guidance has been one of the most precious experiences I've ever known.

I can't tell you how much I miss going even one day without God's voice whispering, *Go left, go right . . . Easy now, that person's tender. Yes, that's the way. Okay, good. Let's take on the next challenge.*

I can't imagine having to "guess" at what I should do. I couldn't bear the loneliness of feeling that I could only talk to myself. The God I'm looking for—and maybe the God you're looking for—is a God who guides us in the everyday activities and interactions of life.

We Need a Guide

Our staff was in the middle of a planning session for our midweek service and we began discussing what people might need prayer for.

"Employment," one person suggested.

"Financial concerns," another offered.

"There are some people with medical problems," a third person chimed in.

"Let's have everyone stand who is facing a pressing decision," someone else offered. There was a moment of silence.

"You think someone will stand for *that*?" a staff member asked.

"I think we ought to give it a shot," another member said.

So the next Wednesday I stood up in front of the church and asked, "How many of you are facing a pressing decision? I'm not talking about a casual one—whether you should buy the dress now or wait to see if it goes on sale, or how you can finagle a nine o'clock tee time on Saturday morning—I'm talking about a critical decision, one that will have severe repercussions on you or your family for many months to come."

To our staff's surprise, over half the congregation stood up. *Over half!*

Many of us are at a crossroads. It's been said that the decisions we make, make us, and to a large extent, that's true. A life well lived is a life full of good decisions. A tragic life is often littered with ill-considered judgments.

Consider your average high school reunion. At my twenty-fifth, I was amazed at how many vibrant, optimistic, and enthusiastic seventeen and eighteen year olds had somehow stumbled into a world of multiple divorces, financial calamities, family estrangement, and vocational nightmares before they had reached the age of forty-five.

Where was the fork in the road that led to such disasters? What highway do you take to travel from the would-be business mogul to the debtor who borrows money in a desperate attempt to stave off his creditors? What bypass leads a proud, loving father of a newborn son to look on the same son—now in his adolescence—with frustration that borders on disgust?

Now, there were many people at my high school reunion who were enjoying the fruit of their good choices. But it was frightening to contemplate those who had been carried away on the riptide of unwise decisions.

The point I'm making is, *we need a guide.* In a world as confusing as ours, we need someone who can look down from on high and say, "Hey, you better go left! There's trouble on the road up ahead!"

God Guides

You can barely read a page in the Bible without encountering a situation where God is guiding someone. Noah was told to build a boat, and he was told exactly how to do it. Abram was instructed to leave his country and go to a land that God would show him. God guided Abraham's servant so that he could locate a wife for Isaac. Israel was led on their journey out of Egypt by a pillar of cloud by day and a pillar of fire by night.

Many of the little-known passages of the Old Testament are often strikingly detailed examples of God's guidance. To a primitive culture, God was saying, "If you get sick, this is how you get well and protect others from becoming infected. If you get hungry, this is what you can eat. If you want to worship, this is how you worship."

When it came time for Solomon to build a temple, God gave him very specific instructions, down to the measurements of the temple utensils. Even Jesus sought guidance! Before choosing His disciples, He spent an entire night in prayer.

The book of Acts could just as well be entitled "The Book of Guidance." First, the apostles are guided to wait until they are empowered with the Holy Spirit. Next, after two apostles are imprisoned, God sends an angel to guide them out of jail. Before appointing deacons, the apostles sought and received God's guidance. Philip is instructed by God to go to a place where he could minister to an Ethiopian official. Ananias is guided to go pray for the persecutor Saul, who would eventually become the apostle Paul. Peter is guided to enter the house of Cornelius, even though doing so was in complete contradiction of Jewish tradition.

On and on we could go, demonstrating the dynamic aspect of God's guidance. Isaiah 58:11 says, "The LORD will guide you continually." Psalm 25:12 adds, "Who is the man that fears the LORD? / Him shall He teach in the way He chooses."

It is guidance like this that makes our Christian faith come alive. I was driving my kids home one time and they started doing all the things that kids do to push a parent to the edge of sanity. They were picking at each other, raising their voices, kicking the seats, the works. I was growing tired of it, and eventually, I let them have it. I went through first gear: "I've about had it with you . . ." I went through second gear: "Furthermore . . ." Then I jumped straight into third gear: "And besides that . . . !" Finally I reached the high-pitched fourth gear: "And one last thing . . . !"

My tirade lasted until the car was parked. Having blown my fuse, my voice grew steadily louder as I sternly told the kids, "Go inside, get ready for bed, go straight there, don't pass go, don't collect two hundred dollars"—that type of stuff.

My daughter, Shauna, walked by and said almost casually, "I'm sorry about that, Dad." Todd, however, who was just seven at the time, has a particularly tender heart. He started crying, managed to choke out how sorry he was, and then just about shattered my soul when he gingerly stretched out his little hand to touch my arm.

In that moment, God just leveled me. Todd's reaching out for my arm was really a kind of question: Was there any love left in my heart for him? I had been too harsh, and I knew it. The Spirit of God broke through my anger to chasten me: *Be careful, Bill. You've got to confront misbehavior, but not that way. Can't you remember how graciously the heavenly Father has treated your misconduct?*

Ten minutes later, I went into Todd's room and said, "Todd, you were wrong to behave the way you did in the car."

"I know, Dad, I know—"

"Let me finish," I broke in. "But I was wrong too. I was way too severe with you. Will you please forgive me?"

Todd wrapped his tiny arms around my neck and wouldn't let go. That kid's thirty-second hug meant the world to me. And it came as a direct result of listening for and receiving God's guidance in something as practical as parenting.

The same God who guides me throughout my day wants to guide you. Let's spend a few moments talking about how we can receive this guidance.

■

Getting God's Guidance

The first thing we have to do to receive God's guidance is to *reevaluate our current guidance systems.* Have you ever been on a commercial airline flight and heard the flight attendant say, "All computers, cellular phones, and electronic games must now be turned off"? The reason she says this is because the

■

electronics that power your computer or Game Boy might interfere with the electronic guidance of the airplane. And competition between guidance systems—especially when you're twenty thousand feet in the air—usually leads to trouble!

The same is true in our life when we have competing guidance systems. Some of us are guided by the philosophy, "I will choose whatever course in life is easiest and causes the least pain." Others are prone to say, "I will opt for the riskiest path." Still others might say, "I will let the people around me choose my path."

Perhaps some of us aren't even consciously aware of why we make the decisions we do, and maybe it's time to decide that we're no longer going to be guided by the easiest path or the riskiest path or the most popular path. Maybe it's time to make the commitment that we're going to take the path that God leads us to take. Proverbs 3:5–6 says, "Trust in the LORD with all your heart, / And lean not on your own understanding; / In all your ways acknowledge Him, / And He shall direct your paths."

The second step to receive God's guidance is to *develop wisdom*. Some of us are our own worst enemies when it comes to seeking God's direction. We misread Proverbs 3:5–6 to mean that God wants us to be weak and dependent in all our decisions. That's not true. God wants to guide us in a way that makes us mature and wise.

Once a man I know was forced to confront a childhood pain that could only be described as apocalyptic. It started innocently enough. This man and his little boy were working on a project together, but he caught himself instinctively making sure that he handed all the tools to his son. For some reason, he was adamant about coaching his son to do the job rather than simply doing it all himself. As they worked together, the father suddenly was overcome by an emotional upheaval that confused him.

Later, he went off to a quiet place and tried to figure out what switch had been flipped. And then he remembered that every time he and his father had worked on a project, his dad had never let him do the work. After just a few minutes of diligent effort, his father always stepped in with a brutally condescending tone and said, "Son, just hand me the tools."

Because his father did all the work, he felt diminished every time he tried to build or fix something. As a grown man, however, this man had learned his lesson, and he was doing the exact opposite with his son, saying, "Here, Son. I will give you the tools and coach you about how to use them. I will patiently guide you, but you must do the actual building so that you can become capable and confident over time."

God has this same attitude with us. He doesn't delight in weakness masquerading as dependence. There's a subtle-but-significant difference between those two realities. I've met many people who, when they get to a crossroads, pray, *Oh, God, give me a vision—and give it to me* now. When nothing happens, they pick up their Bibles and pray, *Oh, God, let this Bible fall open to the answer,* and then they open up their Bible and read an entire page about how many cubic feet the courtyard of the temple was supposed to be.

In near desperation, they pray, *God, send someone to me who has a word from You that they can share with me and tell me what to do.* The entire day passes and no one speaks to them, so they lay their heads on the pillow at night and suddenly get mystical. *All right, God,* they pray, *I desperately need a dream. Just tell me what to do!*

In the morning, the only thing they can remember is that they still don't know what to do. With a sigh of despair, they rummage through their pockets, find a coin, and start flipping.

That's not how God wants us to live. To such people, God responds, "I don't want to guide you that way. It makes you stay weak and dependent in an unhealthy way. If I guided you that way, you'd be no different from a small child or even an unintelligent animal!"

God's plan for our guidance is for us to grow gradually in wisdom before we get to the crossroads. The wisdom of God says, "Back all the way up, as far as you can, before you get to the decision. Then, as you approach the crossroads, look for the signposts along the way that I will use to guide you to the right destination."

Signposts? Yes, signposts.

Signpost Number One: The Bible

Now, I know what a lot of you are thinking. As soon as I tell you that the first signpost is the Bible, you feel an irrepressible urge to yawn. "Boring! Come on, Hybels, can't you give us something a little flashier than that?"

But I would be remiss if I didn't point you to the surest, most productive, and most effective way to receive God's guidance—the Bible. Almost all that we need to know is right there. Often the only things missing are the details. God has already told us in general terms how He wants us to live, love, talk, take care of our bodies, handle our money, pray, function as a family member or employee, and any number of other issues.

I'm sometimes struck by how many of the decisions we face are really no-brainers. The course of action is clearly laid out for us in the Bible. If someone were to say to me, "Shall I sell my house, take all the money, and buy lottery tickets?" I could say with absolute confidence, "God would give you a big 'No' to that one." The Scriptures are clear about "get-rich-quick" schemes or attempting to earn our livelihood through games of chance.

If someone in business agonizes over whether he should tell the truth to a prospective customer or lie, that's another no-brainer. He doesn't have to spend all day agonizing at the cross-roads, trying to figure that one out. He should tell the truth.

If you are a Christ-follower, should you marry someone who is not a part of the family of faith? Second Corinthians 6:14 says very clearly "no" (for reasons that become painfully obvious over time).

The clearest, most direct route to the guidance of God is through His revealed Word, the Bible. We ignore it at our own peril. But sometimes we need more specific guidance on how to *apply* Scripture, and for that, God gives us His Holy Spirit.

Signpost Number Two: The Witness of the Holy Spirit

The second signpost God gives to us is *the witness of the Holy Spirit*. Whereas *obedience* is the catchword with Scripture, *belief* is the catchword with the Holy Spirit. We need to believe in the guiding power of the Holy Spirit, which Jesus promises in John 15:26.

Now, this form of guidance might make some of you feel a bit apprehensive. You're not alone. Lots of people are unnerved about the ministry of the Holy Spirit, but it doesn't have to be that way. Trust me on this one—visions and audible words booming out of the clouds are *not* His usual methods. (I've never experienced either.) God tends to lead us *through gentle spiritual promptings*.

I *have* experienced this. You've read many such incidents throughout this book, but one of the most important occurred twenty-some years ago when I was on the road to being a businessman. My major in college (the first two years) was economics and business administration, and my intent was to follow in the footsteps of my father and eventually get involved in the family business.

The Holy Spirit gave me an unmistakable pull when He led me to help a friend build a youth group. This was a radical departure from my earlier plans, but I followed His leadership and planned to serve in youth ministry for the rest of my life. But then the Holy Spirit began quietly prompting me again, this time to start a church in a movie theater (I laughed, too, when the thought first hit me).

Some of you might ask, "Well, what's that like, Bill? What kind of feeling did you have?" The best way I can describe it is that the Holy Spirit usually gets your attention by creating a sense of unrest in your heart. That sense of unrest should cause you to slow down and listen for promptings. Then, after you receive the prompting, mull it over carefully and prayerfully. If you discern a growing sense of peace that this leading really is from God, start walking in that direction. As you're walking, try to be aware if the peace you felt is growing more solid. If so, keep walking; if not, slow down.

Sometimes we make it sound more difficult than it is. After all, God created us and He knows us better than anyone knows us. He is clearly able to communicate to each one of us in such a way that we can understand Him.

Let me add one caveat here: New Christians in particular need to be very careful about this kind of guidance. A guy told me one time that "God is calling me to quit my job and go down and stand on the street corners of Chicago to preach to people. And He also told me that someone would take care of my wife and kids financially."

I looked at this man and loved him for his sincerity and willingness to take a risk, but grieved over his lack of wisdom and understanding of the Scriptures. The Bible specifically states that if we do not provide for our family we are "worse than an unbeliever." I had to gently tell that man, "I fear you have your wires crossed." If the Holy Spirit was really nudging him, God probably would have added confirmation about how his family's needs could be met. God will usually not ask us to behave like spiritual schizophrenics and prove our "faith" by deliberately violating a fundamental commitment in another area of our lives.

Unfortunately, some of us hear a story like this and throw the baby out with the bathwater. We vow that we will never expose ourselves to these mystical promptings. That's tragic because if we ignore them, we are going to miss out on the very dimension of God's guidance that makes Christianity such an adventure.

Signpost Number Three: The Advice of Wise People

The third signpost is *the advice of wise people*. Proverbs 24:6 says, "For by wise counsel you will wage your own war, / And in a multitude of counselors there is safety." Proverbs 12:15 puts it a little less cryptically: "The way of a fool is right in his own eyes, / But he who heeds counsel is wise."

The writer of Proverbs recognizes that most of us are diligently trying to become the type of people God wants us to become and to accomplish the work God wants us to complete, but often we have spiritual blind spots that derail our progress. God often keeps us on the path by guiding us through the counsel of friends and trusted spiritual advisers. (I could write an entire chapter on how God has used people in my life to encourage me, rebuke me, and assist me in understanding God's guidance in my life.)

Now, we need to be careful. Every church has its share of "self-proclaimed counselors," the kind of people who are unrecognized by the leaders of the church but who love to inflict their opinion on you. Such counsel is often worth approximately what it costs—nothing.

We also must avoid the trap that leads us to expect too much by the way of counsel. Perhaps unconsciously we might think, "God won't tell me what His plans are, so I need to go find a wise Christian who will tell me what to do." This leads us back into the "weak and overly dependent" trap. Please be careful.

The responsibility to make a decision remains on our shoulders. The more healthy approach is to talk to several people who we know are wise and godly, and say to them, "Look, you've been around the spiritual block, and you have more experience in this area than I do. You know God and you know me. You know my biases and blind spots. Can you give me some input?" Then, upon hearing their counsel, consider it carefully and decide how much weight to give it.

Notice I said people (plural), not person (singular). I have learned the hard way that my life is better served by having multiple spiritual mentors instead of a single one. All of us—

even the most mature—have our weak areas, and the beauty of the body of Christ is that you can "pick and choose" according to your need. Think of the church as a smorgasbord of wisdom!

For example, my theological mentor for twenty-five years has been Dr. Gilbert Bilizikian. He offers me better theological mentoring than anybody I have ever met. But when I am trying to figure out what to do with my kids, I call a particular man in my church who is the best father I know. If I have a financial decision to make, I talk to yet another person. If I'm lacking emotional clarity, I spend a session with a wise Christian counselor.

This should be common sense. My eye doctor can advise me about corrective lenses, but I don't ask him how to plot a winning strategy for the next sailing regatta. On the other hand, I don't ask my sailing mentors how I can reconcile the book of James with the writings of Paul.

Get all the good advice you can, but remember that good advice is just one of the signposts. There are others we need to consider, such as signpost number four—our unique design.

Signpost Number Four: Our Unique Design

God often reveals His direction for our lives through the way He made us. The marvelous truth behind this is that God began guiding us even before we were born! By creating us with a certain personality and unique skills, He already set our paths in motion.

Psalm 139:14 says we are "fearfully and wonderfully" made, but it doesn't say we are all made *alike*. You're a one-of-a-kind, handmade original with gifts, skills, and talents different from those of anyone else in the history of civilization.

Greg Ferguson is one of our church's lead vocalists and songwriters. He and I frequently work out together and often talk while we run. One day, I asked him about how his work-day had gone. Greg spent the next several minutes describing his day. He sings for radio and television commercials and does studio recordings in downtown Chicago, but as he talked, my legs got weak. We have an honest relationship, so I was able to say, "Greg, I would hate your job!"

Greg responded with, "Well, what did *you* do today?" So I took him through my day—the study, the meetings, the strategy sessions, the budget planning—and he said, "Well, I would hate your job! You couldn't pay me a million dollars to do that."

You know what? I think God was smiling during our conversation. In fact, I bet He was absolutely *delighted* that two Christians recognized that their Creator gave them different gifts and desires.

I love what I do—and the fact that Greg wouldn't like it doesn't change that one bit. And vice versa.

Recently I was flying home on an airplane and the pleasure of my calling swept over me. I bowed my head and prayed, *God, I cannot imagine being in a place that is more a match for who You made me to be. There is so much challenge at Willow Creek. There is so much creativity and life. I just love it. Thank You for leading my life exactly as You have!*

If I tried to make a go of it in Greg's profession, however, I would be hating life. (And so would everyone who had to listen to me sing!)

We each need to ask, "God, how does the way You made me fit into this decision? Is this going to be a 'fit' with whom You made me to be, or is it going to result in nothing but frustration for everyone involved?"

One of the most dynamic leaders in the New Testament is the apostle Paul. Fortunately for us, we get to meet Paul before he becomes a Christian and this provides us with a good understanding of his personality. Paul was intense. When he got committed to something—watch out! As a sincere Jew, Paul could be expected to keep an arm's length from Christians. But Paul was the zealous type. His goal was not just to avoid contact with Christ-followers. He wanted to *wipe them out!* Then he met Christ on the Damascus road.

After his conversion, do you think God would take someone with Paul's intensity and guide him to dust the shelves in a seminary library? I don't think so. God directed Paul to go out into resistive places and plant churches that would change the lives of people in those communities—and essentially redirect the entire course of history. Now, this assignment would have broken a milder mannered person, but it energized Paul. God's path for his life was perfectly suited for how he had been wired up.

We need to bring the awareness of our uniqueness to our decisions. Our personal makeup is one of the more significant signposts that contributes to God's overall guidance.

Putting It All Together

What do we do after we've accepted God's guidance, applied Scripture, waited for the leading of the Holy Spirit, talked to wise counsel, and inventoried our own character, but still aren't sure where God is leading? Let me give you just a few additional tips.

First, if a decision must be made, *proceed with your own judgment.* Matthew 10:16 tells us to be "wise as serpents and harmless as doves." Make the best call you can with the amount of guidance you have. God might be holding back a little to wean you off a weak and ill-considered dependence. You might also find a clue at a crossroad by reading Psalm 37, which promises that God will give us the desires of our heart. If you have honestly sought God's guidance and given Him time to speak, and yet you still draw a blank, you might simply ask yourself, *Since I know this decision doesn't have a clear scriptural directive, what do I want to do?* Your desires might be a legitimate indicator of what direction to go.

Second, *remember that feelings of bliss do not necessarily confirm God's leading.* I've heard people say, "I know God led me into this job, but I'm making less on commissions than I did in my last job, and I don't know what's going on! Maybe I made a mistake." Some Christian leaders are led to start churches, and after five years there is still only a struggling core of people doing their best to survive. Does that necessarily mean they missed God's call?

God does not promise that obedience immediately leads to success or bliss. Sometimes, obedience can lead to very difficult challenges. Obedience led Jesus to the cross. Obedience led Paul to go to Jerusalem, even though he knew he'd probably be killed. Paul even said, "I know what the will of God is—and it is going to be excruciatingly painful—but I will follow His guidance, no matter what!"

Third, *enjoy the search.* I meet with people all the time who hate to be in the tension of not knowing the will of God, and they desperately leap into any sort of resolution that appears to present itself. These are the type of people who want to know what college they're going to by the time they're sophomores in high school and want to know who their spouse will be by the time they become college seniors.

Life doesn't always work that way, so enjoy the adventure of receiving God's guidance. Taste it, revel in it, appreciate the fact that the journey is often a lot more exciting than arriving at the destination.

There was a period of six months at Willow Creek I didn't have a clue about where God was leading our church. At board meetings I'd say, "I wish I could give you a better sense about where I think God wants us to go, but to be honest, I simply don't know." Thankfully, our leaders were okay with that. In fact, they pulled together and prayed and brainstormed with one another, and eventually God's direction became clear to all of us. Looking back, that was an exciting era.

Finally, *find comfort in God's providence*. Some of us tend to overdo the implications of making a wrong choice. God is a good guide, but He's also a good "fixer." Romans 8:28 says, "And we know that all things work together for good to those who love God, to those who are the called according to His purpose." This doesn't mean we should be cavalier about decision making, but it does mean that, after seriously considering all the signposts with which God guides us, we can have confidence that God can teach us and grow us up, even if we take a wrong path. And since God can make new paths and create new highways, we'll never be totally locked into a place where God can't reach us. We might have to suffer a few (or many) negative consequences, but even then, we won't suffer them alone. God will be right there with us.

The God we're looking for doesn't hide His guidance in the stars. He doesn't conceal it in a crystal ball. He isn't capricious like the flip of a coin. He guides us in such a way that He makes us grow and makes us wise and makes us mature over time. He guides us down paths that lead us into the kinds of relationships and vocations and churches that give Him honor.

This is all part of an incredible journey—the journey of walking with a God who is all-powerful, all-knowing, and always present; who is gracious and righteous and who keeps His commitments; and who guides us every step of the way.

10

WHO
ALWAYS GIVES?

"Jenny" was a beautiful young woman: personable, competent, self-confident, dynamic. As we talked, the topic of marriage and family came up. "Is that something that you foresee in your future?" I asked. "Or do you pretty much plan on just building a career?"

"Oh, no," Jenny said. "I would *love* to meet someone and be in a committed relationship that might lead to marriage. That would be wonderful, if it happened, but I seriously doubt that it ever will."

"Why?" I asked, startled by her certainty that she could never find someone to marry. I couldn't imagine her having any problem attracting a mate.

"I've dated a lot of men," she said, "and I've come to the conclusion that all men can be put into one of two categories: the givers and the takers. So far, all I've met are takers, and I have no intentions of hooking up with a taker."

I remembered that conversation when I was enjoying one of our family's annual summer breaks in Michigan. During these precious weeks, I'm "incognito." Few people know I'm a pastor. Hanging out around the marina, the beaches, and the boatyards, I usually have many opportunities to build friendships and sometimes to share my faith.

One day I was talking with a guy I had met about all that Christ had done in my life, and I brought the conversation to its close by saying, "You know, Bob, a relationship with Christ is available to you as well. All you have to do is open up your heart and tell God that you need Him, and you, too, can start a whole new life."

Bob looked as though I had just invited him to have lunch with me on the moon.

It wasn't the first time I'd seen a response like that. Even so, I periodically still find it puzzling. God has given me so much that I find it difficult to fathom why anybody doesn't want to get to know Him. I'm so proud of who He is, I'm so cognizant of how gracious He is to people, that sometimes it catches me off guard when somebody informs me he's simply not interested.

As Bob and I discussed his reluctance, the "sticking point" became crystal clear: In Bob's mind, God was clearly a taker rather than a giver. Bob had done the calculations and he had ended up believing that he would lose much more than he would gain if he gave his heart to Christ. *God is a demanding Being*, he thought. *God has a lot of rules and He forbids a lot of fun.*

Like Jenny, Bob was asking himself, *Who wants to hook up with a taker?*

■

The God Who Gives

To be candid with you I'm somewhat embarrassed that we even need to have this discussion. Trying to prove that God is a giver is sort of like trying to prove that Billy Graham is an evangelist, that John Grisham is a writer, or that Michael Jordan can play basketball. It should be so obvious that no discussion is needed.

Unfortunately, conventional wisdom still sees it the other way. If after this point in the book, you're still a seeker, it may be that, like Jenny, you're wary of hooking up with a "taker," and that, like Bob, you still see God as a taker.

If that's you, hold on. We've got a lot to cover. Throughout Scripture, we're taught that, among other things, God's generosity is *wonderful* and that *it continues on into eternity.*

God's Generosity Is Wonderful

Ephesians 1:6 says, "Now all praise to God for his wonderful kindness" (TLB). Notice, Paul doesn't say, "minimal kindness." He isn't suggesting that God's kindness will do in a pinch if no other kindness is available. On the contrary, God delights in lavish giving. When people receive a thoughtful gift, they are moved. When they encounter God's unsparing and abundant gift, they are left breathless and amazed, saying, "What a God. What an outlandishly generous God."

His Lavish Gifts

During my daughter's freshman year at college, she got a severe case of mononucleosis. We actually had to move her home from the West Coast. For seven weeks she was flat on her back, but as she started to gain a little strength, she began

■

sneaking into my office and leaving sticky-notes all over the place. I found them under the phone console, on top of my desk, and in my briefcase. The notes said, "I love you, Dad" or "There has never been a little girl who loved her dad more." Those notes were everywhere I turned.

Her lavish affection of love wiped me out. I still remember sitting in my office chair and just shaking my head thinking, *What an amazing thing to have a daughter who has that kind of love for me. What a gift!*

Our God does that sort of thing routinely—His sticky-notes are everywhere. He paints the autumn leaves for you, and He says, "I love you." He answers prayer, and He says, "I love you." He strengthens you when you're weak, and He says, "I love you." When you worship in your church and you have a holy moment, He says, "I love you."

For many years now I have spent time early in the morning returning thanks to God for His generosity toward me. I often scratch the following initials in my spiral notebook, which I record my prayers in: S. A. S. S.G. H.S. E.L. WCCC. They stand for salvation, adoption, sanctification, spiritual gifts, the Holy Spirit, eternal life, and Willow Creek Community Church. Each day as I write out these letters I feel a deep sense of gratitude to the Lord for His generosity to me. Beyond these manifestations of His goodness follows a list of material blessings and relational blessings, which I thank God for one by one. By the time I finish this part of my prayer routine, I am freshly awed by God's amazing generosity.

God gives these gifts to us with joyful liberality. And according to His promise we can count on them in the future.

God's Giving Is Continuous

By *continuous*, I mean that God doesn't run out of generosity. Lamentations 3:23 says God's mercies are "new every morning." God's kindness is not like the sunset—brilliant in its intensity, but dying every second. God's generosity keeps coming and coming and coming. When you wake up tomorrow morning, there will be no less generosity to greet you than there was the morning before. Ten years from now, God's generosity will still be knocking people over with its lavishness.

The last verse of the hymn "Amazing Grace" says:

When we've been there ten thousand years,
Bright shining as the sun,
We've no less days to sing God's praise
Than when we'd first begun.

One of the most difficult things about life on earth is that almost as soon as something good starts to happen, it's over. You look forward all week long to a visit from some old friends; the next thing you know, they're headed out the door, saying "good-bye." A bride-to-be dreams for months about her wedding—but the ceremony is over in less than an hour. Parents get excited about giving the kids their Christmas presents—but the sounds of paper tearing and children squealing are silenced before breakfast.

That's *not* the nature of God's generosity. *Ten thousand years* after the celebration starts, we won't have used up any time at all! God's generosity will extend all throughout eternity.

Are you starting to get a grasp of what I'm saying? From the moment you meet the true God, you will discover that He is a giver. The more you learn about Him and the longer you live in relationship with Him, the more frequently you will find yourself on your knees worshiping Him for His incredible generosity.

But somewhere along the path of your spiritual journey, you will awaken to another realization about God: He wants to turn you and me into generous people. He wants us to become givers. And that's a tall order for some of us.

Transformed into a Giver

Many years ago, our daughter Shauna got a sliver in the palm of her hand. The splinter hurt, but when Shauna saw the needle and tweezers we had taken out to remove it, she got the impression that the cure would be worse than the injury, so she kept her tiny five-year-old fingers clamped shut.

To get the splinter out, Lynne and I had to pry back each of her fingers, then hold them open while I moved as quickly as possible to remove it. If we allowed Shauna to keep her hand closed, the cut might have become infected. To heal her, we had to get her hand open.

God faces the same dilemma with us. He knows that most of us by nature are tightfisted people. He knows we will experience a deep, satisfying kind of joy when we open our hands to the needs all around us, but to show us that joy, He often has to pry back our selfish fingers, one by one.

How does He do that? We have a case study in Luke 19 when Jesus opened the hands attached to a "clutcher" named Zacchaeus.

Zacchaeus had an advantage over most clutchers by being "employed" as a tax collector. In those days, tax collectors had the official license to become legal extortioners. They were allowed to charge you the government's going tax rate, *plus* whatever percentage they thought they could get out of you. If you didn't pay the tax as well as their own take, you went to jail.

Zacchaeus went into a dinner with Jesus bearing all the signs of a man who has clutched his fist so tightly, it was practically frozen that way. Yet before Zacchaeus put down the napkin used to wipe the last bit of food from his lips, he had vowed to begin giving half of his earnings to the poor.

What happened? Jesus opened Zacchaeus's heart, He opened his mind, and then He opened his hands.

Open Heart, Open Hands

We are not given all the details of what was discussed between Jesus and Zacchaeus, but I think Jesus probably said something like this: "Hey, Zach, your heart and your hands are clasped around the wrong things. Your heart should be wrapped around loving God and loving others, and your hands should be open to give and receive love, but you're so obsessed with clutching money that your heart's longing can never be met."

Then I think Jesus stunned Zacchaeus with some mind-blowing generosity. Maybe He told Zacchaeus about how He would willingly open up His hands and receive the Roman spikes on Zacchaeus's behalf, and how He would remove the lifetime's worth of wrongs that painfully pricked Zacchaeus's conscience. And then, perhaps, Jesus began talking about the gift that a lonely, ostracized clutcher would value most of all:

"After I have sacrificed My own body and blood on your account, I am going to adopt you into My family. I will offer Myself as One who will personally see to it that your prayers are answered. And when you die, I'm going to give you a place in heaven so magnificent that it will make a king's palace—which you so clearly covet—look like the hovel of your poorest victim."

Just imagine, for a moment, that you are Zacchaeus. Imagine being the man whom everyone hates to see coming their way. Little kids whisper when you walk by. The faces of wives and husbands turn red with anger every time you knock on their door. When you turn your back, you hear the muffled expletives cast your way, followed by sadistic threats.

And then a Man tells you He'll not only be your friend, but He'll treat you like a member of His own family. And not only will He meet with you—you who have spent a lifetime having doors slammed shut in your face—but He'll do so publicly, even at the risk of alienating His supporters. And then He'll take your punishment and pay for it Himself.

You know you've done nothing to earn this Man's favor. You know you've lived in such a way that He would be fully justified to treat you as an enemy, or at the very least, to ignore you. But He's been so generous with His love. He's been so generous with His time. And He's talking so generously of the future that you're absolutely stunned.

At some point in this conversation, the enormity of Jesus' generosity melts the stubborn heart of Zacchaeus. His hands loosen just a little. They may not open completely, but the knuckles aren't so white, the fingers aren't curled quite so tightly. Zacchaeus imagines himself a different person. And that's when Jesus moves to the second step: He further opens Zacchaeus's hands by opening his mind.

Open Mind

Once Zacchaeus's heart was softened, Jesus began renewing Zacchaeus's mind. I think maybe, just maybe, Jesus led

Zacchaeus to an Old Testament text in the book of Ecclesiastes. Solomon, one of the smartest and wealthiest men who ever lived, wrote, "I enlarged my works. I built houses. I planted vineyards. I made gardens and parks. I planted in them all kinds of fruit trees, and even made ponds of water to irrigate a forest.

"I collected silver and gold and the treasures of kings, and then sat back to ponder all that my hands had done. When I considered the energy it had taken to obtain all this, I concluded that all of it was wasted. It was chasing after the wind and all of my possessions were as worthless as a moldy piece of bread."

I think maybe Jesus went on to personalize Solomon's teaching. "Zacchaeus, something has got to change in your mind about the nature of 'stuff.' It never delivers all that it promises. Even after you secure more of it than you ever could have dreamed, you'll still have a hole in your soul."

Maybe He ended this little session by exposing the economic cycle of insanity. That's when a person orients his life around the acquisition of money and material goods, succeeds at it to some degree, and then comes face-to-face with the fact that it never completely satisfies.

"Let's say, Zacchaeus, that what you really wanted was a camel. You stayed up at night thinking about how much easier your life would be, traveling from village to village, if only you had a camel to ride on.

"And then, one day, you had earned enough to buy that camel and you did so. Curiously enough, scarcely a week had gone by when you found yourself lying awake once again because you began thinking about buying a new coat. It gets cold at night! And how much easier life would be if only you could earn enough to get that new coat, so you turn the screws on one family here, another family there, and finally you extort enough money to buy a new coat.

"Will that be enough?

"Does it stop there?"

Zacchaeus is sweating now. This prophet is telling his story! *He knows!*

Jesus goes on. "Rather than looking heavenward and saying, 'God, help me manage this money in such a way that it does not tyrannize and ruin my life,' you think about how nice it would be to have a larger home. You keep buying and spending more, which then raises the bar of what has to be earned the next year. So you work a little harder, take a few more risks, inwardly wince at what you have to do to get ahead, and pretty soon you're out of control.

"Zacchaeus, I'm telling you, it's insanity. Marriages suffer, spiritual lives suffer, character suffers, and pretty soon, a vibrant, fully alive image-bearer of God gets reduced to an earning-and-spending machine. You deserve to be more than that, Zach.

"It is fine to have some 'stuff,' Zacchaeus. God won't begrudge you your camel and your coat. But when money becomes the preoccupation of your life and you fix your heart on it, it will leave you disappointed every single time."

Slowly, Zacchaeus's mind grasps the wisdom of Jesus' words. Zacchaeus feels something shift inside of him. He makes new plans. Instead of lying awake at night plotting ways to extort more money, he vows, with the eager voice of a child, to find new ways to give some of it away. "Fifty percent of all that I have I am going to give to the poor!" he announces. "I will also give back four times to anybody I have cheated."

With a softened heart and a renewed mind Zacchaeus's hands were finally opened. But now what about yours? Are you ready to become a giver?

Your Hands

When you look at your hands do you like what you see? Or do you wish your hands looked a little bit more like the open hands of Christ or Zacchaeus? Don't start wringing them just yet. Remember, if God needs to change your hands, He doesn't usually start there. He starts with your heart, and that means He wants to overwhelm you with His own generosity first. It's His nature to be generous, and He wants it to become ours. The transformation begins to happen when we first open up our hearts to His goodness.

I was on an airplane coming back from the West Coast once and a flight attendant slipped me a note from someone who was sitting several rows behind me. The note said, "I saw you on the plane, but I didn't want to bother you. You have no idea what Willow Creek Community Church has meant to me. Just a few years ago I was making a lot of mistakes with my life. I was addicted to my job and it was ruining my marriage and pushing away my kids."

In other words, this man was living with a closed fist. He wasn't giving his wife the affection she needed. He wasn't giving his children the affirmation and relationship that they craved. But by a strange set of circumstances, he wound up at church and was surprised by grace.

In his closing paragraph, he said, "We have never met. I don't know if we ever will. But you need to know that the love of God has not only changed my heart"—that's the start!—"but it has reunited a broken marriage and has brought our kids back into our family."

When God touched his heart, his hands fell open and his family was put back together. Now, he viewed everything differently. That's the way it works. God starts with the heart, and then He transforms our minds.

That's what happened to my dad many years ago. As his heart was warmed toward God, he began thinking about ways he could give something back to Him. Dad owned some land in northern Michigan and decided to donate it to our church— and Camp Paradise was born. Thousands of lives have been transformed over the last twenty years at that beautiful retreat.

Maybe you don't have a couple of hundred acres to give. But what do you have? And are you willing to give it?

I've found that, maybe once or twice in someone's life, God will ask His children to make a high-risk, sacrificial gift that, when you first think of it, causes you to grab your seat and wait for your breath to return.

That's what happened to a woman in Jesus' time. This is the powerful narrative of a true giver, the type of giver God wants us to become.

A Sacrificial Gift

What does a woman do after she decides to quit her life as a prostitute? The Bible tells the story of one such woman whose first act as an officially unemployed person was to literally pour her life savings over the head of Jesus. She took a jar of costly perfume and lovingly applied every drop to the Man who had shown her the way to eternal life.

This was not the cheap stuff you find in the Dollar General Store. This was the kind of perfume that you walk by at

Nordstrom, look at the price tag, and say, "Yeah, like if I wanted to spend a month's salary . . ." Yet she gave it, every drop, not knowing how she'd earn a living in the future.

One time I felt this challenge toward "maximized giving." God prompted my heart toward a particular need, and there was no doubt in my mind that He was instructing me to "max out" and literally give everything that I could. This is not the pattern that God usually calls us to. Normally, God calls us to give out of wise, consistent stewardship, but on this occasion, I believed God was asking me to cash out everything and give it to Him.

When I wrote that check out, my hands were shaking and I felt like a man who opens his eyes only to find out he's walking over Niagara Falls on a tightrope. But gradually a deep sense of peace and satisfaction flooded my heart.

In the next weeks and months I watched as God miraculously began resupplying our needs. I also realized through that experience that God didn't need my money as much as He wanted to open my hands. Like five-year-old Shauna, I had kept clutching my fist, and God wanted to remove my "sliver"—the hold that financial security can have on all of us—and slowly, finger by finger, manage to pry my hands open. The freedom was exhilarating. Let me tell you—there is no "high" like the elation and joy that come from a sacrificial act of obedience.

If you want to be truly happy, you won't find it on an endless quest for more stuff. You'll find it in receiving God's generosity and then passing that generosity along.

I know that the God you're looking for is a giver, not a taker. You don't want to hook up with a taker, and I don't blame you. But the God we're talking about, the God of the Bible, the God I love, is a God who gave His only Son for our benefit—and that was just the start!

Every time we take a breath, enjoy the taste of a well-prepared meal, smell the glory of a spring morning, frolic in the pleasure of a hearty laugh, or experience the intimacy of a lifelong friendship, we don't have to guess where that gift came from: "The eyes of all look expectantly to You, / And You give them their food in due season. / You open Your hand / And satisfy the desire of every living thing."[1]

And now I've got some equally good news to share with you. This will never change. God will never cease giving. How can I know that? Read the next chapter, and you'll find out.

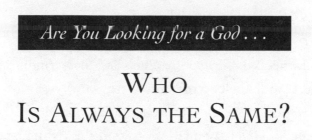

11

Are You Looking for a God...

WHO
IS ALWAYS THE SAME?

There's something about struggle and conflict and mutually shared effort that forges an intense bond. Few relationships carry the intensity of the life-and-death partnership of soldiers, or even the exhilaration of a successful season among athletic teammates. Why else would veterans continue to celebrate a few short years of their life with regular reunions? Why else do high school buddies immediately begin talking about the "big game" or the risky prank years after it happened?

I've discovered that sailing regattas do more than prove the worth of a boat and its crew; they also create relationships that would be impossible to forge on dry land. In the type of races we sail, we're dependent on everybody doing their job, and doing it right. One missed maneuver, one sloppy tack, and our boat could lose precious seconds and even the entire regatta.

Not all of the men who race on my boat profess faith in Christ, but the struggles we've faced, the victories we've shared, and the bitter disappointments we've overcome have all combined to create a very meaningful bond.

One man in particular, however, has about as much interest in spiritual things as teenagers have in jobs. This past summer I came down to the dock and he ran to meet me before I got to the boat.

"Bill," he said, "thanks so much for the sermon tape you gave me. It really helped me out!"

I was shocked! "You?" I asked, dumbfounded.

"Yeah, look!" He pointed up toward the rigging and I saw that he had taken the tape out of the plastic case, cut it into strips, and made "wind tellers" out of it. "It really helped me out!"

The rest of the guys laughed and gave me a hard time. "Hey, Bill, when the wind gets *really* strong, maybe we'll be able to hear your voice!"

I suppose for some of you who may still be seekers at this point, this book may not be any more helpful to you than my cassette tape was to my sailing buddy. Before you make that final decision, however, I want to leave you with one last thought, something you may not have considered: Your world is changing. Every day, everything around you, from the number of hairs on your head to the wrinkles on your face; to the relationships you cherish, to the job that you endure; it's all changing.

To which you might respond, "So what?"

You may not think you need God now; you may actually be coping fine, all things considered, but there will come a time in your life when you need just the type of God we've been describing, and when you do, please remember this: He hasn't changed. He won't change. Everything I've said in this book will be as true twenty years from now as it is today.

In a world kept chaotic by change, you will eventually discover, as I have, that this is one of the most precious qualities of the God we are looking for: He doesn't change.

■

The Trauma of Change

It was one of the most difficult encounters I've ever faced, and I've faced some big ones. I've had to comfort parents who had just lost a child; I've helped married couples patch up the emotional devastation of an affair; I've held the hand of a church member who was dying of cancer. But this was one of the most painful of all.

My wife and I had taken in two children for a kind of foster care and a tight bond soon developed between myself and the little eight-year-old boy. The child stayed with us for several months, and we were starting to see some good things happening in his life.

On one particular occasion Ronnie and I spent several hours out in the garage, working on a model car. He was very excited about the project, and I watched him as he treated the car with an almost reverent respect. He wanted everything to fit and look perfectly, and we took our time to get it just right.

As the project continued, I got the phone call I knew would eventually come. (Why did it have to be now?)

I went back out to the garage, where Ronnie and I had resumed our efforts on the model car. Praying for the right opening, I finally said, as tenderly as I could, "Well, Buddy, in a few days we're going to have to make a different arrangement

■

here, because the people who make these decisions are going to ask you to move again."

After I spoke these words, a frightening coldness passed over Ronnie's face. I could see the tension begin to work its way through his jaw. He was silent, but the emotions were clearly churning inside. Perhaps I shouldn't have been surprised, but I was—he slowly but determinedly raised his fist and smashed it into his prized model car.

Five minutes earlier, such an act would have felt sacrilegious, but that was before his archenemy—*change*—had blown its hideous breath his way.

He backed up against the garage wall, as if he couldn't get far enough away from his smashed car, and shouted, "What do people think I am, a football? They throw me here and they throw me there, and they kick me around all over the place. I'm sick and tired of being a football!"

This precious little guy was literally lost in a windstorm of change. As soon as he thought roots were sinking into the ground, he was yanked up and planted somewhere else. His schools changed, his neighborhoods changed, his houses changed, even his "parents" changed. Sometimes things changed for the better, sometimes they changed for the worse, but what he hated more than anything else was change itself. He was at a point where he'd even choose a *bad* situation as long as he could stay in one place for a while.

Do you ever feel like that, wishing you could just hold up your hands and scream, "Time out!" and make everything stop?

Do you know how many times I've sat in a counseling room and a spouse pointed a finger at his or her life partner and shouted, "You've changed! You're not the person I married!"?

Do you know how many times I've talked to employees who loved working for their company—maybe they've even worked there for several decades—and the company gets bought out and the people change and the mission changes and the atmosphere changes and all of a sudden the employees mournfully reminisce about the "good old days"?

Countries are reconfigured and entire governments are ousted in a carefully executed coup. NFL quarterbacks grow "old" at age thirty-six and retire; statesmen die; matriarchs pass on. We are lost in a sea of change. As soon as we think we've learned how to parent babies, we have to learn how to discipline toddlers. When we get really good with toddlers, we've suddenly got preadolescents; when we get really good with preadolescents, we've got these strange creatures called teenagers. We never quite catch up.

Just because our team won the World Series last year doesn't mean they'll win it this year. Even worse, just because a friend was true or a spouse pledged her love doesn't guarantee that that loyalty and pledge will be honored ten years from now.

Things change. *We* change. Experts tell us the most successful people are the ones who learn to cope with change. But I'm convinced the best way to cope with change, ironically enough, is to get to know a God who doesn't change, One who provides an anchor in the swirling seas of change.

■

Our God Doesn't Change

When I was growing up, I remember seeing the Scripture verse written above a church pulpit: "For I am the LORD, I do not change."[1] And I remember thinking that such a statement

■

was at once the most obvious and least relevant statement I had ever read in all my life.

"You got that right", I said to myself. "God doesn't change." The church doesn't change. The choir doesn't change. So what? Big deal! What does that have to do with me?"

One of my problems was that I had a completely wrong understanding of what the "immutability"—or unchanging-ness—of God really means. I assumed it meant that God was frozen, static, and unwilling to budge. Everything around Him changed, but He didn't change, and maybe because of that He was becoming ever less relevant.

But then I came across a passage in Scripture that obliterated my misunderstanding of the immutability of God. In Genesis, chapter 18, Abraham has a fascinating face-to-face discussion with God. Taking Abraham into His confidence, God reveals His plan to wipe out Sodom and Gomorrah because of their wickedness. When Abraham learns that the Lord intends to destroy his nephew's adopted hometown if a certain number of righteous people can't be found, he gets a little nervous. Abraham had done business in Sodom. He had walked the streets of Gomorrah. He knew that if their future depended on righteousness, their lease on life was about to expire.

In a desperate attempt to hold back the inevitable, Abraham starts a conversation with God. "Hey, God, You wouldn't destroy the righteous with the wicked, would You? What if there are *fifty* righteous people living in those towns? You wouldn't display Your wrath on fifty righteous people, would You?"

God carefully reconsiders. "No," He says. "If there are fifty righteous people in Sodom, I'll spare the city for their sake."

Then Abraham starts counting all the righteous people in Sodom and Gomorrah he can think of. After three individuals, he's stumped—but he's still forty-seven away from fifty! Abraham then proceeds to "bargain" God down to saving the cities on the basis of forty-five righteous people, then forty, then thirty, then twenty, and finally, ten righteous people.

I was blown away the first time I realized the full implication of this. Does this mean we have a God who changes plans? Do we serve a God who will react to prayers and respond to the requests of humans? *Maybe I don't really understand the nature of this immutability business*, I thought.

I found that the immutability of God, whatever it means, doesn't rule out a God who is responsive and who is willing to react to our problems and requests. We're not merely living in a deterministic world. We have a God who moves and acts and reacts. Yet, at the same time, we have a God who is absolutely consistent in His character.

■

God Is Absolutely Consistent in His Character

The fact that God is absolutely consistent in His character is good news, but only because of the quality of His character. Sometimes consistency can be bad. I know plenty of dishonest, slothful, deceitful people. In their situations, consistency is a huge problem.

But when we're talking about God—His power, His presence, His knowledge, His commitments, His graciousness, His generosity, and the rest—it becomes very clear that *any change would have to be for the worse*. If God changed, that would mean He would have to be less gracious. He would have to be less

■

faithful. He would have to speak to me less and guide me less, and I don't want that, do you?

I may want my spouse to change, I may want my children to change, and I may want my friends and my church to change—I certainly want myself to change—but I don't want God to change.

Think about it. Any product can be improved. You can create a laundry detergent that makes clothes whiter and is better for the environment. You can improve your favorite breakfast cereal by adding more vitamins, more fiber, or more crunch, but how can you improve on omniscience? How can you improve on omnipotence? How can you improve on perfect righteousness? The only way God can change is to be less than He is, and the Bible is adamant that that will never happen: "With whom [God] there is no variation or shadow of turning."[2]

Notice, not only is there no turning, there isn't even a *shadow* of turning. God doesn't even begin to *lean* away from righteousness, much less move His feet. He's consistent. In a world where everything changes (and that usually means everything decays) God stands firm in every aspect of His character.

This is right where immutability begins to touch our lives in a powerful way. In spite of Scripture's teaching, in spite of centuries of Christian experience faithfully passed on through the ages, I still have my moments when I begin to doubt things about God. Sometimes when the pressures in my life are building, I whisper to myself, "I don't think God knows about this." He may be omniscient, but somehow, this has escaped His attention.

Or we get ourselves in a tricky situation—disaster seems certain and God seems distant—and we say in fear, "I don't think He is present with me right now. This may be the first time He's taken a fifteen-minute break, but finally, it's happened."

Or we get ourselves buried in an addiction or entangled in a destructive relationship, or we see a loved one trapped by seemingly insurmountable adverse circumstances, and quietly we groan, "God may be all-powerful, but I don't think even He has the power to solve this one."

Maybe we say to ourselves, "The God of Moses who parted the waters; the God of David who slew Goliath—that was a God in His prime. But somehow, over the years, the centuries have taken a toll on God."

Some of us fear that maybe God has "lost His stuff." His fastball doesn't pop like it used to. His curveball hangs and His breaking ball just doesn't break anymore, and those of us left out in the field are powerless to dodge all the hits that now come flying our way.

To which God would cry through the prophet Malachi, "For I am the LORD, I do not change."[3] God has been omniscient from eternity past and will be to eternity future. God will always know everything about you. He will always be present. Every time you step on a plane, you can rest secure that God is on *your* plane. He isn't staying home more these days. He's not taking an occasional day off. He has not lost His stuff.

Everything that God was, He is, and we can benefit immeasurably from this precious truth. The same God who empowered Samson, Gideon, and Paul seeks to empower my life and your life, because God hasn't changed. This is great news for the committed—but it's sobering news for the complacent.

Bad News for the Complacent

While committed believers may find comfort in God's unchanging nature, others may fervently hope that God has mellowed over the years. Perhaps you think that, though in the

Old Testament God showed a mean streak, He softened somewhat in the New Testament, and now, two thousand years later, He simply looks down and smiles, saying, "Well, boys will be boys and girls will be girls—I guess they've all been pretty good this year."

Let me be straight with you: God doesn't hate sin with any less passion than He hated it ten thousand years ago. You won't be judged any differently from Adam and Eve, because God doesn't hold us to different standards. His standard has been, and always will be, perfection: One sin and you're accountable for it.

That's the deal.

Don't think you can "slide" by a God who's a little less vigilant these days. That simply won't happen. If you've committed that one sin and haven't crawled into the spiritual protection plan of Jesus Christ, you are exposed in a way you don't want to be exposed.

In Washington, D.C., as in many cities, the major highways all have "car-pool" lanes. If you drive in these lanes during peak hours and don't have the required number of people in your car, you're going to be out sixty-five dollars if you are caught. Sometimes, however, if there's a bad accident or it's a legal holiday, the restrictions on these car-pool lanes will be lifted and anyone can use them. At other times, drivers simply take a chance. They dart in and out of the restricted lanes, hoping that no police car will show up in their rearview mirror. Not so with God.

His restrictions are *never* lifted. He doesn't change His rules according to the calendar or any particular generation. He doesn't make exceptions for particular challenges. God won't say, "That's okay, spew your anger onto your entire family.

You've had a rough day at work. I understand. This time, your sin won't count against you."

This is a scary thought, isn't it? But remember, the same God who never changes His laws also never changes His free offer of grace, love, security, and blessing.

Unchanging Security

When Todd was about five years old, he climbed into my bed early one morning, and we spent a few minutes talking. As was my custom, I pulled him close to me and said, "I love you, Bud."

"I love you, too, Dad."

Then I decided to add something new. I said, "You know, I'm going to be crazy about you for the rest of your life."

"You mean even when I get older?"

"Yep, Bud, even when you get older."

"Even when I'm, like, thirty?"

"Yeah, Kid, even when you're thirty. I'll still be crazy about you."

As Todd drifted off to sleep in my arms I said a prayer for him. *Please, Son, don't ever waste one moment of time worrying about whether I'll ever stop loving you.*

Yet I've wasted so many hours wondering when God was going to stop loving me or being gracious to me or blessing me. Malachi 3:6 and James 1:17 promise me that I will not be the first person that God fails. That person will never exist, and it's nothing but a colossal waste of time for us to worry about it.

This unchanging security provides us a solid rock in a world full of uncertainty. Have you taken a look at a ten-year-old globe lately? From the fall of the Soviet Union to the changes in Africa, we live in a world that shows no sign of consistent national boundaries. Have you ever studied a ten-year-old book on astronomy? Recent satellite discoveries have moved us way past what we knew just ten years ago.

In virtually every realm of academia and science, knowledge becomes outdated about as quickly as it can be written down.

But this study of the God we're looking for is a study for the ages. If the English language as we know it is decipherable two thousand years from now, somebody ought to be able to pick up this book and get just as much benefit from the character and unchanging nature of God as the person who reads it in the waning years of the twentieth century.

The reverse is also true. What was written for us thousands of years ago is just as true today as it was then. Since we know all about this God we're looking for, some of you may now be asking, "Well, then, what does this God want from me?"

The gods of the ancient pagan world would respond, "Give us your firstborn children and burn them in the fire." The gods of other religions might respond, "Make sure you obey all the rules." But the God we're looking for responds in a way that might surprise you. The God we're looking for says, "Give Me your heart. Hold out your hands. Put on your shoes. Let's walk through life together."

■

Walking with God

Back in the eighth century B.C., Israel began wondering, *What does God want from us, anyway?* They started thinking about several possibilities, and—no surprise here—they came up with all the wrong answers. (We all do, when we try to answer spiritual questions apart from God's Word.)

Into this mass confusion, God dropped a prophet named Micah. As part of his teaching, Micah spends some time echoing all of Israel's misguided speculations:

With what shall I come before the LORD,
And bow myself before the High God?
Shall I come before Him with burnt offerings,
With calves a year old?
Will the LORD be pleased with thousands of rams,
Ten thousand rivers of oil?
Shall I give my firstborn for my transgression,
The fruit of my body for the sin of my soul?[4]

There's a little bit of sarcasm at play here. It's sort of like someone saying, "Wait a minute, what does God really want? A ten? No, well how about my life's savings? Not enough, huh? Still not enough? Well, then, what will satisfy Him? How about I give Him Microsoft, IBM, General Motors? Fine—if that's not enough, I guess I'll just give Him my firstborn child. Maybe then He'll be satisfied!"

Micah concluded that none of these would suffice. The person asking them completely misunderstands the nature and character of God. None of these things could possibly satisfy God's heart.

Well, then, what *does* God want? Micah provides a very simple answer that still applies today: *He wants us to walk with Him.*

That's right. Just walk with Him.

Micah explains:

He has shown you, O man, what is good;
And what does the LORD require of you
But to do justly,

To love mercy,
And to walk humbly with your God?[5]

Recently I was looking through a family scrapbook and saw a picture of my daughter Shauna and me when she was a wobbling one year old. We were on the beach in South Haven, Michigan, where we have spent part of our summers for most of our lives. I was young and she was very young, and I was bending over so we could walk hand in hand along the water's edge. She was ambling along in that wrap-an-entire-hand-around-one-finger stage, and I was ambling along in the mystified bliss of a young father who couldn't believe God would entrust him with a child so precious.

Recently, my daughter and I went back to South Haven— the same beach, but I went there with a very different child. Shauna, who is now twenty, said, "Let's go for a walk, Dad." We walked along the beach, hand in hand, and talked. All of a sudden, I remembered the photograph and the thought struck me forcefully, *We've been walking this stretch of beach together for twenty years.*

What gave that moment so much power for me was not that I had walked on the beach for twenty years—it was *whom I had walked with.* The companionship created the meaning.

I remembered back to the time when I had to drive Shauna to school. We were listening to a news report about an orphanage while she played with the power locks and windows.

"You better watch out, Kiddo," I said playfully, "or I'm gonna drop you off at an orphanage."

A beautiful and mischievous smile slowly worked its way across Shauna's face. She scooted over toward me, and said, "Ah, Dad. You wouldn't last five minutes."

She was right, of course. She had called my bluff perfectly. If we had been playing poker, she would have wiped me out. She knew that our companionship was one of the greatest delights of my life!

And now, several years later, it was her companionship that made this beach walk so meaningful. What is there about walking that knits our hearts together? A walk is what lovers do when they want to be together. A walk is what bonds the generations of fathers and daughters and mothers and sons. A walk is what husbands and wives do when they just want to be close to each other and enjoy each other's presence.

And a walk is what Christ-followers do when they want to be in a loving relationship with God. All of us are going to walk our eighteen years or thirty-six years or eighty years or maybe even one hundred years on the "beach" of this life, but whose hand will we hold? Whose fellowship will we enjoy along the way?

The answer to that question will make all the difference.

So what does the God of the universe want to do with us? He's saying, right now, "Let's go for a walk. Here's My hand. Let's do life together."

What does it mean to walk with God? It means that when I wake up in the morning, my first conscious thought is, *Good morning, God. I'm glad You're in my life.* When I'm getting ready for work, God gently reminds me that there's more to "today" than quotas, deadlines, or sermons. There are people to be touched, wrongs to be righted, needs to be met, joy to be spread, and love to be given and received.

During my morning commute in the car, I might slide in a worship tape so that I can just relax and think about Him.

As I go through the rest of my day, God points things out to me. I might say something I regret and He'll squeeze my hand. I'll respond, "Yeah, Lord, I know, I know." And He'll say, "Good. Let's get it straightened out, beginning with the 'I'm sorry.'" And when I do, He'll squeeze my hand and say, "Good. Now let's keep going."

I don't want to be a self-absorbed person, but truthfully sometimes I get busy and forget God for a time. That's when God reminds me to slow down and refocus. Recently, I was half-walking, half-running from my office to the church's farthest seminar room to meet with some leaders. I had my schedule all planned out, including how long it was going to take me to walk, and how fast I was going to have to walk to make it on time.

When I got partway there, I saw someone from our building services staff washing a window with the enthusiasm of a man who's just been given a life sentence. I remember thinking to myself, *If this is a contest between the rag and the window, the window is winning.* I was planning to walk right by, but I could sense God squeezing my hand and whispering, *Stop. Just ask him how he's doing. It looks like he's hurting.*

So I stopped and I said, "Are you okay?" He looked at me and his eyes said, "I'm not, but I know you're always busy. And if I start telling you what's breaking my heart and you say, 'Gotta go, bye—' it's going to be too hurtful for me."

God squeezed my hand—a little harder this time—and said, *Let the other meeting wait,* so I spoke to the man once again and added, "I'm not in a hurry. What's up?" And what came out was a kind of hurt that only a couple of us on the staff could identify with. So I spent the next twenty minutes encouraging him and praying for him.

Later on, as I reflected on that moment with God and the man by the window, I realized that that particular staff member has probably heard hundreds of my sermons. Yet years later, when he looks back and reflects on the impact that my life had on his, he probably won't remember many of them. But he will probably remember the day I stopped to talk when the window was winning.

If I hadn't been walking with God that day I never would have felt Him squeezing my hand or heard Him telling me to stop. I would have walked right on by, and both that man and I would be poorer because of it.

When I walk with God, and I'm on my drive home from work, God might whisper to me the kinds of things I need to remember to be a good parent to my kids and a loving husband to my wife. If I listen carefully, the rest of my evening will be transformed, and there's a good chance that my entire family and I will fall to sleep with a smile on our faces, rather than with an ache in our hearts.

When I finally put my head on the pillow, I'll say, *Well, I didn't hit home runs all day, but I walked with You, God, and I did some things right. It was wonderful. Thank You.*

If you don't understand what I'm describing, you don't fully understand Christianity. I don't understand it completely either but at the core of who God is resides a yearning to go through today and tomorrow and forever with *you.* Yes, *you.* He longs to love you, and guide you and nurture you and correct you and forgive you and provide you with enough grace and strength to meet every challenge that comes your way. If you don't live today that way, you're denying yourself the most precious part of what it means to be fully alive.

Too many people fail to understand what I'm about to say, so I want to say it to you directly. Take a breath so you can catch the full force of this next statement. Are you ready? Here it is: *The God you're looking for is head over heels in love with you.*

Let me give you some more soulwarming news: His affection for you is bound up in who He is, not in what you do, so His affection for you will *never* wane. Because of that love God wants to walk with you today and He'll want to walk with you tomorrow, and the day after that, and the day after that, throughout eternity.

And when we truly walk with God throughout our day, life slowly starts to fall into place. I'm not saying that life will go perfectly or even smoothly. But I am saying that we'll gradually experience the fulfillment of Jesus' promise in John 10:10: "life in all its fullness"(TLB).

Please allow me one more sailing illustration to tie together everything about relating to the God we're all looking for.

■

The Rock Star and the Regatta

It was our biggest regatta of the year: the 1996 Great Lakes Championship. In this series of seven races, all the boats in our class gather together to fight it out and determine who is champion in our fleet.

In other words, you get bragging rights for 365 days.

This was not a regatta to treat lightly. This was not the event to gather crew from the "whoever is warm and willing" file. This race calls each boat owner to pull together his absolute best talent.

Now through an unusual set of circumstances I have enjoyed a growing friendship with John Bertrand over the last five years. John is a professional sailor who has competed in the America's Cup and who is generally recognized as one of the top sailors in the world, a real-life "rock star." (Professional sailors at his level are called rock stars.) By class rules, each boat is allowed one rock star. On a wing and a prayer, I decided to fax him an invitation to serve as the tactician on our boat, even though doing so was a little bit like asking Michael Jordan to play on a park district basketball team.

To my surprise and delight, John agreed to come.

Now, imagine you're at your pickup game on a public basketball court and Michael Jordan walks into the gym. You get to smile at the other guys and say, "He's with us."

I couldn't wait.

John flew in the day before the regatta, and right away I was treated to a clinic on how to do things right. Every habit of mine—in sailing and leadership—was challenged as I watched a master at work.

As soon as John got into my car, he pulled out the crew list and said, "Tell me about every person on your crew. How good are they? What are their personalities? Where are they strong? What are their weaknesses? What motivates them? I need to get to know them if I'm going to encourage them and teach them."

The next thing he asked about was our boat and equipment. "Are we fast, or are we slow? Is the boat prepared? Is the rig tuned? How are the sails?"

Next, we went over the competition. "I want to memorize the names of the top four or five boats," he said. "I need to know where the lead boats are the whole race and how we can put them behind us."

From there, we discussed our crew. "What do we do best? Are we good at starts, good at tacking, good at mark roundings?"

To watch how an internationally renowned sailor approaches a regatta served me well. I realized that John didn't get to the level he has achieved by accident; he had a plan all laid out and he was very intentional about it.

Once we were out on the water, I was likewise challenged. The normal procedure while running the starting line is to do a wind check once or twice. You head your boat into the wind, use a compass, and find out where the wind is coming from to determine how to approach the starting line. Before the first race, John had us do about ten wind checks, and he kept doing them throughout the day. Under John's tutelage, we did at least seven wind checks before each race.

From his example I realized—and this is important—to compete at the highest levels you must work harder and leave less to chance than everyone else.

Once the races started, John was unapologetic in asking the crew to do our best. Before one maneuver came up, I remember him saying, "All right, we're going to be tacking up here, and I need it to be the best tack you've ever done." As soon as the tack was completed, the praise was immediate. "Great tack, guys, great tack."

Then, the time came for all of us to jump up on the rail where we sit to hike out. John's voice cut through the wind: "Are you hiking out your hardest? Can you give me a bit more?"

Hearing him ask for our best was very inspirational to me. I realized I never go home from a day of leading and working at church feeling good if I've frittered any time away. The days that I feel best are the days when I know that God got my best.

When each race was over, right after the finish gun would sound, John would get up and go to every person on the crew and individually thank them for their efforts. This didn't surprise me when he did it the first time, but I took notice when he did it for all seven races.

When we got back to the dock, John further amazed us by helping us clean up the boat. As a general rule, rock stars don't do cleanup. They don't haul sails, they don't do repairs (they may do some photo ops and sign some autographs but no grunt work). But once we were back at the dock, John stayed on the boat, just like the rest of us, and asked, "What needs to be fixed? What needs to be hauled? What needs to be cleaned?"

You might be wondering by now how we did. We scored six first places, and one second place. Since you're allowed to throw out one race, we won the regatta with all first-place finishes, the first time in the history of our fleet that that had been done!

As our boat came back from the race course, other crews teased us by waving their hands and calling out, "We are not worthy!"

Well that's what happens when you get Michael Jordan— or John Bertrand—on your side.

That day was exhilarating for me. I don't know how many hours I have logged on the sea—far too many to count, certainly. But I will never forget the few days spent with John.

The same can be true of life in general. We're all putting in our hours, but are those hours prisons of frustration or windows of opportunity? That's when I realized that walking with God is a little bit like sailing with John Bertrand. You still have to work, you still sweat out a few tacks and turns, you still make a few mistakes, but you're a different person having somebody so knowledgeable and capable on deck—and it's absolutely exhilarating.

You never have to sail alone another day in your life. You can sail the high seas of this life from crisis to crisis, alone in your boat, or you can sail with the God who not only knows how to handle the waves, but who rules over them. He's all-knowing, ever-present, and all-powerful. He doesn't keep you guessing—He's an expressive God and a passionate Friend. He'll act as a refuge in all your storms. He'll be a gracious and generous companion whose commitment to you will be unparalleled. You'll never have to worry about waking up and finding that He's jumped ship. He'll guide you through every season, and He'll never lead you astray.

Isn't this the God you're looking for? Isn't this the God you need? If, after all this you're still a seeker, can I make one final suggestion? Give God a chance, just one chance. Maybe you can do what a friend of ours did. My wife and I have been trying to help a woman and her husband understand who Christ is and what He's really like. And one morning the wife decided to give God a chance by attempting to communicate with Him.

It began very innocently. She woke up and thought, *I can do it right now, so I will.* Here's what she wrote to us in a letter:

This morning I talked to God. I hadn't planned on doing this. But the house was quiet, my husband had left, and I just started talking to the Lord. I've never done this really. Of course, as a young person, I did the rosary with my grandmother and knew all the words to the "Hail Mary" and "The Lord's Prayer," but this was different. I said those things because I was supposed to. This morning, for some reason, I *wanted* to talk to God.

She ended her letter by saying,

> As I talked with God, I must admit I felt uncomfortable, vulnerable, scared, and yet somehow greatly relieved. I know I'll talk to God again soon. I'm telling you this because I trust you guys and I know you're both rooting me on.

The awkwardness, the "strangeness," even the fear, is all to be expected when you first make the acquaintance of a new friend. But she's getting it. She's beginning to understand.

What about you? What's your experience like?

You know, I'm pretty sure that I could lose everything—including my family and friends—and I could survive. It would be excruciatingly painful, of course. But maybe after forty or fifty years of recuperation time, I might manage a smile now and then. Yet I could never go back to CEO Christianity. I couldn't survive a single day without the friendship of Christ, not one single day.

Sooner or later everybody looks for God. I really believe that the God of the Bible, the God I love is the God you're looking for. You might be at the top of your game or buried deep in a merciless valley, but whether it's success or failure that opens your eyes, I believe you're going to find God through a life-changing relationship with Jesus Christ.

The good news is: He's not hiding. He's right here. He's ready to take your hand and walk through this life, and the next, with you.

It's your move.

NOTES

Chapter 1
1. He knows the ordinances of heaven (Job 38:33), the sun and the moon (Ps. 104:19), and the clouds (Job 37:16).
2. Matt. 10:29.
3. Matt. 10:30.
4. Ps. 139:2.
5. Ps. 56:8 TLB.
6. Matt. 6:4.

Chapter 2
1. John 4:24.
2. John 15:15.
3. Psalm 139:7.
4. Psalm 139:8.
5. Psalm 139:11.
6. Psalm 34:18.

Chapter 3
1. Jer. 32:27 NASB.
2. Job 26:12, 14.
3. Ex. 9:16.
4. Ex. 14:31 NIV.
5. Eccl. 8:8 NIV.
6. Judg. 3:12.
7. Judg. 14:6.
8. Acts 4:33.
9. Phil. 3:10.
10. 1 Cor. 2:5.
11. Acts 3:12.

Chapter 4
1. Zeph. 3:17.
2. John 15:11.

3. Matt. 26:38.
4. Matt. 26:38 TLB.
5. Heb. 10:27.

Chapter 5
1. Josh. 20:2–3.
2. Jer. 20:7, 8 NASB.
3. Jer. 20:14–15 NASB.
4. Jer. 20:11, 13 NASB.

Chapter 6
1. Ps. 11:7.
2. Ps. 119:137.
3. Ps. 111:3.
4. Ps. 119:47.
5. Quoted from William Kilpatrick's *Why Johnny Doesn't Know Right From Wrong* (New York: Touchstone Books, 1993).
6. Ibid.
7. Ibid.
8. Rom. 6:18.

Chapter 7
1. Eph. 2:8–9.
2. John 10:10.
3. Ps. 116:12.

Chapter 8
1. Gen. 12:2–3.
2. Gen. 15:3.
3. Matt. 6:34.
4. Rom. 3:24.
5. 1 John 1:9.
6. Matt. 6:33.
7. From Matt. 5:13.
8. Acts 17:6.
9. Acts 21:28.
10. Gal. 3:28.

Chapter 9
1. Prov. 27:6.

Chapter 10
1. Ps. 145:15–16.

Chapter 11
1. Mal. 3:6.
2. James 1:17.
3. Mal. 3:6.
4. Mic. 6:6–7.
5. Mic. 6:8.

ABOUT THE AUTHOR

Bill Hybels is the founding pastor of Willow Creek Community Church in South Barrington, Illinois, and is chairman of the board of the Willow Creek Association. He is the bestselling author of *Honest to God, Too Busy Not to Pray, Rediscovering Church,* and *Descending into Greatness* and is coauthor of *Becoming a Contagious Christian* with Mark Mittelberg.

Look for these other resources by Bill Hybels

Becoming a Contagious Christian

Bill Hybels and Mark Mittelberg

Becoming a Contagious Christian is a proven action plan for impacting the spiritual lives of those around you. Based on their own experiences, the authors' powerful stories will help you get rid of your misconceptions about evangelism and develop your own "contagious" Christian character.

Softcover   0-310-21008-9

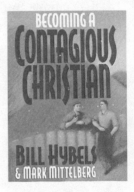

Fit to Be Tied
Making Marriage Last a Lifetime

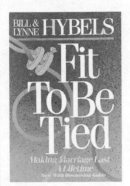

Bill and Lynne Hybels
Writing openly about their own marriage, Bill and Lynne Hybels give a biblical perspective to the realities of married life. From understanding your spouse's temperament to ways of courting creatively, this book gives honest, helpful insight into developing a healthy, loving Christian marriage.

Softcover   0-310-53371-6
with discussion guide

Available at your local Christian bookstore.

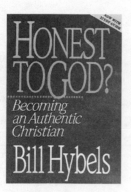
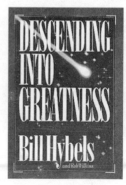